THE

VOICE

OF

GOD

HOW HE SPEAKS TO US TODAY

DAVID PETTS

Published by www.davidpetts.org

ISBN 978-1-4709-8372-7

JESUS SAID:

> *I am the good shepherd. The good shepherd lays down his life for the sheep*
>
> *…the sheep listen to his voice*
>
> *…his sheep follow him because they know his voice*
>
> *…they will never follow a stranger; in fact, they will run away from him because they do not recognize a stranger's voice.*

Selected from John 10:1-11

To Eileen

my darling wife

with gratitude for your love

friendship, wisdom, faithfulness and patience

over sixty years of marriage

About the author

David Petts grew up in a Christian home and gave his life to Christ at the age of fourteen, shortly after which he preached his first sermon. Now, seventy years later, he's still going strong.

After several years in pastoral ministry, he served as Principal of Mattersey Hall Bible College from 1977 to 2004. He has also served as President of the European Pentecostal Theological Association, Vice Chairman of the Pentecostal European Fellowship, and as a member of the Presidium of the Pentecostal World Fellowship.

His teaching ministry has taken him to over forty different countries where he has preached in churches, colleges, and universities around the world.

The author of several books, he has now made available over 200 podcasts details of which may be found on his website.

A former Exhibitioner of Brasenose College, Oxford, David's academic achievements include an MA, an MTh, and a PhD in Theology. He is an Honorary Academic Fellow of the University of Wales.

He is married to Eileen who has been a strong support to his ministry for over 60 years. Their three children are all married and actively involved in Christian ministry.

Further information may be obtained from his website: www.davidpetts.org

Foreword

As I look back over 70 years of Christian experience, the most exciting thing I have discovered is that God has a plan for my life. Yes, even though I am now almost 84 years old, God still has a plan.

He has a plan for you too, and the most important thing you can possibly do is find out what it is. God loves you. He wants what's best for you. He knows you better than you know yourself. So it only makes sense to ask him for guidance. Besides, if you're already a Christian and love Jesus, you'll surely *want* to do what God wants you to.

This book is about how God *speaks* and how he *guides* us. It will help you to recognize his voice, to know when he is speaking to you and when he is not. I'll be telling you what I have learnt from personal **experience**. I'll be telling you how he spoke to me through a book that I found on top of my parents' piano on the very day that I been told it was out of print and how that book changed my life. I'll be telling you how God spoke to me in the middle of the night in January 1972 and radically changed the direction of my ministry.

But more importantly I'll be sharing with you from what the **Bible** teaches. The Bible is God's inspired word and it's the Bible itself that is the main way God speaks to Christians today. Everything we experience must be judged by what the Bible has to say on the matter. God won't contradict himself by saying something through our experience that is not in line with what he's already said in the Bible. So when I share my experience of how God has guided and spoken to me, I'm just using it as an illustration of what the Bible teaches.

We'll begin with a summary of what the Bible teaches about the many different ways God speaks to us. Then in the chapters that follow we'll expand on the things we've outlined. I believe that the examples I give from my personal experience that will encourage you and inspire you. In fact, it may well be that God will speak to you through the pages of this book. Please have an open heart and mind. It's an exciting thing to know that God is speaking to you.

David Petts

Brixham, Devon

November 2022

Contents

PART FOUR   GOD SPEAKS TO US DIRECTLY BY HIS SPIRIT

PART FIVE   HEARING AND RESPONDING

INTRODUCTION

God speaks in many different ways

There are so many different ways God speaks to us. Let's begin with a brief outline of what the Bible has to say on this important subject. We will see that:

- *God speaks to all humanity through his creation*
- *He spoke to Israel by the prophets*
- *He has finally spoken by his Son, Jesus*
- *He speaks through the Bible*
- *He speaks through other people*
- *He speaks directly by his Spirit*

God speaks through his creation

The Bible is very clear that God speaks to all of us through his wonderful creation. Nowhere in the Bible do we find an argument for the existence of God. Bible writers simply assumed it. The world we live in and the heavens above are clear evidence that a wonderful designer has been at work.

> Psalm 19:1-4
>
> *The heavens **declare** the glory of God; the skies **proclaim** the work of his hands. Day after day they pour forth **speech**; night after night they display knowledge. There is no speech or*

*language where their **voice** is not heard. Their voice goes out into all the earth, their **words** to the ends of the world.*

Notice the words *declare, proclaim, speech, voice, words*. As he looks into the night sky the psalmist sees the stars and planets as speaking to all humanity, to people of every language. They declare the glory of God. They pour forth speech. They are shouting at us that they are the work of his hands. No doubt the apostle Paul had this passage in mind when he wrote in Romans 1:20

> *...since the creation of the world God's invisible qualities - his eternal power and divine nature - have been clearly seen, being understood from what has been made, so that men are without excuse.*

And leading scientist, Francis Collins agrees. As Director of the National Institute for Health in the USA, leader in the scientific response to COVID19, and recipient of the 2020 Templeton Prize, was formerly Director of the Human Genome Project. He led a team of over 2000 scientists who collaborated to determine the three billion letters in the human genome – our own DNA instruction book. He said:

> *I cannot see how nature could have created itself. Only a supernatural force that is outside of space and time could have done that*[1].

There is really no excuse for not believing in God. The creation itself provides abundant evidence that there must be a creator. And today we see more and more television programmes showing how wonderfully designed the creation is. As a Christian I find myself

---

[1] Francis Collins, *The Language of God*, Simon and Schuster UK, 2007, p. 67.

praising God for his skill, his genius, his creativity. I hear phrases like 'this is designed to...', and I rejoice because I know the Designer.

But I groan inwardly when the credit is given to 'Mother Nature' or 'evolution' or even the animal or plant itself rather than to God. In today's society the creation is being applauded rather than the Creator (Romans 1:25). 'Mother Nature' has become a substitute for Father God! Evolution, a blind force, is said to have a purpose! And a plant is described as having a strategy2, implying that it has made a conscious decision to equip itself with an ability to grow in a certain way! No wonder the Psalmist said, The fool says in his heart, 'There is no God' (Psalm 14:1).

For us who believe, on the other hand, the creation speaks eloquently not only of God's existence but of his great and glorious power, his wisdom, his faithfulness, his beauty and his love. God not only speaks to us through creation, he shouts at us!

God spoke to Israel by the prophets

The Bible is very clear, then, that God continually speaks to all people, everywhere, by his wonderful creation. But that is not all. The Bible also reveals that God spoke in Old Testament times to his chosen people, Israel, by the prophets he sent to them. We often think of prophets as people who foretell the future, and it's true that the Old Testament prophets did foretell in great detail the coming of Christ. But that wasn't their primary role. Their main purpose was to tell the people of Israel how they should live and to give them

---

[2] Sir David Attenborough, The Green Planet, BBC Television, Sunday 30th January 2022.

direction as to what they should do[3]. They did this as they were led and guided by the Holy Spirit. The people needed the guidance of prophets because in Old Testament times (and in the New Testament before Pentecost) very few of them had a personal experience of the Holy Spirit. The Spirit was given only to specific people for specific purposes[4], but the day was coming when the gift of the Spirit would be made available to all. Through the prophet Joel God declared:

> And afterward, I will pour out my Spirit on **all** people. Your sons and daughters will prophesy, your old men will dream dreams, your young men will see visions. Even on my servants, both men and women, I will pour out my Spirit in those days (Joel 2:28-29).

This prophecy was fulfilled on the Day of Pentecost when Jesus' disciples were filled with the Holy Spirit (Acts 2:1-4). The disciples spoke languages they had never learned and, when the crowd asked, What does this mean? Peter replied:

> ...this is what was spoken by the prophet Joel, "'In the last days, God says**, I will pour out my Spirit on all people.** Your sons and daughters will **prophesy**, your young men will see visions, your old men will dream dreams. Even on my servants, both men and women, I will pour out my Spirit in those days, and they will **prophesy** (Acts 2:16-18).

The ability to receive God's Spirit, to hear what God is saying and to speak to others on his behalf was to be no longer restricted to a few.

---

[3] For more on this, see *Body Builders – Gifts to make God's people grow*, Chapter 2.

[4] See *The Holy Spirit – an Introduction*, Chapter 2. Available from www.davidpetts.org

As from Pentecost all God's people have the Spirit. We have no need of prophets to tell us what to do! But does this mean that there are no prophets in the New Testament church? Are there no prophets today? There most certainly are. As we'll see in a later chapter, prophets are one of the ways God speaks to us today. It's just that their role is not exactly the same as that of the Old Testament prophets.

The need for that kind of prophet ceased with the coming of the Holy Spirit at Pentecost. In fact the New Testament is clear that the role of the Old Testament prophets was over. Once Jesus had come, God has finally spoken to us by his Son.

God has finally spoken by his Son, Jesus

The letter to the Hebrews begins with this statement:

> In the past God **spoke to our forefathers through the prophets** at many times and in various ways, but in these last days he has spoken to us **by his Son** (Heb. 1:1-2).

What does this mean? As we've just seen, one way God speaks to us is through the Holy *Spirit*. But this verse says that God has spoken by his *Son*. At first sight this might look like a contradiction but in fact it is not. Firstly, it's because Jesus came and died for us that we have the Holy Spirit. He died for us, rose again, and 40 days later ascended into heaven. Notice what Peter says when preaching to the crowd on the day of Pentecost:

> God has raised this Jesus to life, and we are all witnesses of the fact. Exalted to the right hand of God, he has received from the Father the promised Holy Spirit and has poured out what you now see and hear (Acts 2:32-33).

It was Jesus who poured out the Spirit and it is through his Spirit that he speaks to us today.

Secondly, Hebrews 1:2 says that God has spoken by his Son. The Aorist tense the writer uses here indicates that he is referring to a specific period in history – the life, death, and resurrection of the Lord Jesus. The writer is saying that God's final word to the human race has been spoken in Jesus. There's a sense in which God has nothing more to say! There's nothing more to add. The message of Jesus is enough! And God is still speaking to us by it. He speaks through Jesus' teaching, his example, his character, his death and resurrection. Perhaps that's why John's Gospel describes Jesus as the Word:

> In the beginning was the Word, and the Word was with God, and the Word was God. He was with God in the beginning... The Word became flesh and made his dwelling among us. We have seen his glory, the glory of the One and Only, who came from the Father, full of grace and truth. (John 1:1- 2,14).

We use words when we speak. They're our primary means of communication. And God speaks through his Word, Jesus who became flesh and lived among us. But he also speaks through his written word, the Bible.

God speaks through the Bible

If God speaks to us through Jesus, it's obvious that he will speak to us through the Bible which tells us about him. The Old Testament law and prophets pointed forward to him (Luke 24:27). The New Testament Gospels record what he said and did while he was here on earth. The book of Acts records how he continued to work through his disciples by the power of his Spirit. And the letters written to the churches that were formed through the preaching of his disciples give us wonderful teaching about Jesus himself and the kind of lives we should live as his followers. The Bible is God's word first and foremost because it tells us about Jesus.

In later chapters we'll talk in more detail about how God speaks to us through the Bible. We'll see how the word of God reveals to us the way of salvation. He longs to save us. It also teaches us what we should believe and how we should behave. He teaches us. He gives us wonderful promises. He encourages us. What's more, he speaks to us prophetically. He directs us. There are times when a verse of scripture seems to leap out of the page. The Holy Spirit is drawing our attention to it, and through it God speaks very directly and specifically into our immediate situation. There have been several occasions when God has spoken to me in this way, and I'll be sharing some of them with you later.

God speaks through other people

From what we have seen so far it's clear that sometimes God speaks to us directly, without anyone else being involved. This is the case when he speaks to us through creation or when he speaks as we read the Bible. The same is true when he speaks through an inner prompting or through a dream or vision. However, very often he uses other people to speak to us. When we first believed the gospel it was because someone else told us about it. This could have happened by a variety of ways – by witnessing or preaching or writing or singing for example. In fact, this is the main way that God intends the gospel to be spread[5].

---

[5] Romans 10:13-14

And the same is true throughout our Christian lives. He often speaks through other people. If we had Christian parents, God probably first spoke to us through them, although we may well have not realised it at the time! In church we should certainly expect God to speak to us through preaching or teaching or through someone exercising a spiritual gift like prophecy. And it's not just in church! A casual conversation while travelling in a car or on a country walk can turn out to contain a very real word from the Lord.

In all these examples God is using someone else to speak to us. He speaks through them to us, and they may not even realise that he's using them that way! And, of course, he can use **us** to speak to **them**. But that's something we'll talk about another time. In fact, throughout the series we'll be developing in greater detail many of things we've said in this chapter. And there will be some new areas too. So far I have concentrated mainly on how God *speaks* to us. But God also *guides* us sometimes without speaking. As the children of God is our privilege to be **led** by the Spirit[6].

God speaks directly by his Spirit

There are several verses in the New Testament that tell us that the Holy Spirit speaks[7]. As we've just seen, one way he speaks is through the Bible. But at times he speaks independently of scripture. A good example is found in Acts 13:1-3:

> In the church at Antioch there were prophets and teachers...
> While they were worshiping the Lord and fasting, **the Holy Spirit said**, "Set apart for me Barnabas and Saul for the work

---

[6] Romans 8:14
[7] This is most clear in John 14-16 and Acts 13:2

to which I have called them." So after they had fasted and prayed, they placed their hands on them and sent them off.

You'll notice that what the Holy Spirit said was giving a specific instruction. He wasn't on this occasion speaking through a verse of scripture. No Bible verse would be that specific. He was telling the church leaders at Antioch to *set apart* Barnabas and Saul (or Paul) for a particular ministry they already knew he had called them to. After more fasting and praying, they did this by laying hands on them and sending them off on what was to be Paul's first missionary journey.

But how exactly did the Holy Spirit speak to them? The answer is, we don't know. Did he speak with an audible voice? That's certainly a possibility. It seems to have happened that way in Acts 10 when Peter was on the roof top in Joppa. Peter falls into a trance and sees a vision of something like a large sheet being let down to earth by its four corners with all kinds of animals in it. (This included 'unclean' creatures that Peter as a Jew was forbidden to eat under Old Testament law). Then in verses 13-16 we're told that Peter hears a voice:

> *Then a **voice** told him, "Get up, Peter. Kill and eat." "Surely not, **Lord!**" Peter replied. "I have never eaten anything impure or unclean." The **voice** spoke to him a second time, "Do not call anything impure that God has made clean." This happened three times...*

Peter immediately identifies it as the voice of the Lord (v.14) and verse 19 tells us that while Peter was still thinking about the vision, the Spirit said to him, "Simon, three men are looking for you..." So, the Holy Spirit does speak sometimes with an audible voice and it's possible that that is how he spoke to the church leaders in Acts 13:1-3.

However, it's worth bearing in mind that in Acts 10 Peter heard the voice while he was having a vision and we know that **dreams and visions** are one of the ways the Spirit may speak to us. It was through a vision God gave to Paul that the gospel first came to Europe (Acts 16:6-10) and Acts 2:16-17 makes it clear that dreams and visions are to be expected as a result of the coming of the Holy Spirit:

> *In the last days, God says,* **I will pour out my Spirit on all people.** *Your sons and daughters will* **prophesy,** *your young men will see* **visions,** *your old men will dream* **dreams.**

But this passage, as well as mentioning dreams and visions, also mentions **prophecy.** So in Acts 13 the Spirit could have spoken through **a spiritual gift** like **prophecy.** The passage mentions that there were **prophets** in the church at Antioch and perhaps that is the most obvious way to understand it.

So the Spirit may speak with an audible voice, through a dream or vision, or through a spiritual gift like prophecy. But these are not the only ways that God may speak to us. For example, he may speak through angels, or supernatural signs, or by what is sometimes called *an inner witness or prompting,* and we'll be saying more about all these things in later chapters.

PART ONE

GOD SPEAKS TO US THROUGH JESUS

CHAPTER ONE

God speaks to us through Jesus

In the introduction we gave an outline of what the Bible teaches on how God speaks to us. We saw that:

1. God speaks to all humanity through creation

2. He spoke to Israel by the prophets

3. He has finally spoken by his Son

4. He speaks today through the Bible

5. He speaks through other people

6. He speaks directly by his Spirit

Now because I am writing this book primarily about how God speaks to us as Christians today, I won't be developing points 1 and 2 any further. This is because:

1. Although Christians may see more clearly than other people that God speaks through his creation, as we saw in the last chapter, God speaks to **all** people in this way, not just to Christians.

2. The fact that God spoke to Israel in Old Testament times by the prophets has no direct bearing on how he speaks to Christians today. He now speaks by his Son.

It's points 3-6, however, that do have a direct bearing on how God speaks to us as Christians today, and those are the things we'll be dealing with in more detail in the remaining chapters. We'll begin in this chapter by considering how God continues to speak to us by

Jesus. As we have already seen, although in the past God spoke to Israel through the Old Testament prophets, he has now spoken by his Son:

> In the past God **spoke to our forefathers through the prophets** at many times and in various ways, but in these last days he has spoken to us **by his Son** (Heb. 1:1-2).

But he has not just spoken. He continues to speak to us through Jesus. Jesus is God's Word to us (John 1:1-2, 14). In Jesus God continues to speak to us in the following ways:

1. God speaks to us in the person of Jesus
2. God speaks to us in the words of Jesus
3. God speaks to us in the actions of Jesus.

In all these three ways, God is revealing to us what he is like, teaching us what to believe, and showing us how we should live.

God speaks to us in the person of Jesus

We have already seen from Hebrews 1 that in these last days God has spoken to us by his Son. But the passage goes on to make a staggering claim about who Jesus actually is:

> In the past God spoke to our forefathers through the prophets at many times and in various ways, but in these last days he has spoken to us by his Son, whom he appointed heir of all things, and through whom he made the universe. The Son is the **radiance of God's glory and the exact representation of his being,** sustaining all things by his powerful word. After he had provided purification for sins, he sat down at the right hand of the Majesty in heaven (Hebrews 1:1-3).

These verses make it clear that Jesus is none other than God himself. He is the exact representation of his being. Colossians 1 says the same thing:

> For he has rescued us from the dominion of darkness and brought us into the kingdom of the Son he loves, in whom we have redemption, the forgiveness of sins. **He is the image of the invisible God,** the firstborn over all creation. For by him all things were created: things in heaven and on earth, visible and invisible, whether thrones or powers or rulers or authorities; all things were created by him and for him (vv.13-16).

Jesus is here described as the image of the invisible God. Putting it simply, both writers are saying, If you want to know what God is like, take a look at Jesus! Jesus himself said the same thing in John 14:6-9:

> I am the way and the truth and the life. No one comes to the Father except through me. **If you really knew me, you would know my Father as well.** From now on, you do know him and have seen him." Philip said, "Lord, show us the Father and that will be enough for us." Jesus answered: "Don't you know me, Philip, even after I have been among you such a long time? **Anyone who has seen me has seen the Father...**

All these verses confirm the truth that in the person of Jesus we see exactly what God is like. As we have seen, God has revealed his existence through creation and from it we have some understanding of what God is like. But that is nothing compared with the way God has revealed himself in Jesus. In Jesus we have a clear picture of who God is. John 1:18 tells us that

> No one has ever seen God, but the One and Only who is at the Father's side has made him known.

Jesus is the full and final revelation of who God is. To see Jesus is to see God. God speaks to us in Jesus and reveals his goodness, his kindness, his compassion, his humility, his patience, and his love. In Jesus we see him healing the sick, giving sight to the blind, feeding the hungry, raising the dead and forgiving sinners. As we look at Jesus in the pages of the New Testament we hear God saying, I LOVE YOU!

God speaks to us in the words of Jesus

So God speaks to us in the person of Jesus revealing what God is like. But he also speaks to us in the words of Jesus teaching us what to believe. What we believe is important for three main reasons:

- It affects what we say

- It influences how we behave

- It determines our ultimate destiny.

*What we believe is important because it affects **what we say***
Jesus made it clear that what we believe in our heart will **affect what we say**:

> The good man brings good things out of the good stored up in his heart, and the evil man brings evil things out of the evil stored up in his heart. For **out of the overflow of his heart his mouth speaks** (Luke 6:45. Cf. Matthew 12:34).

The apostle Paul expresses the same truth when he says:

> It is written: "I believed; therefore I have spoken." With that same spirit of faith we also believe and therefore speak (2 Corinthians 4:13, quoting Psalm 116:10).

And again In Romans 10:9-10 he says:

> That if you confess with your mouth, "Jesus is Lord," and believe in your heart that God raised him from the dead, you will be saved. For it is with your **heart** that you **believe** and are justified, and it is with your **mouth** that you **confess** and are saved.

These verses are not merely an illustration of how what we believe will affect what we say. They show that, when it comes to the matter of salvation, there's a clear connection between believing in Jesus with our heart and acknowledging him with our mouth. If our faith is real, we'll be talking about him. In the following verses Paul goes on to say that salvation is available to anyone who will trust in Jesus (v.11) and that everyone who calls on the name of the Lord will be saved (v.13). He then goes on to ask:

> How, then, can they call on the one they have not believed in? And how can they believe in the one of whom they have not heard? And how can they hear without someone preaching to them? (v.14).

So what we believe is important because it affects what we say, and what we say is important because it affects other people. If we believe what Jesus says about himself and tell others about him, we will be sharing with them the truth that can lead to their salvation. As we read the New Testament, then, we should pay attention to what Jesus says. His words are the expression of his heart and he himself is the Word of God and is the expression of his Father's heart. God speaks to us in the words of Jesus teaching us what to believe and tell others. On the other hand, if we believe and say things that are not true, we may lead others into error.

What we believe is important because it influences how we behave

We only have to look around us to see plenty of evidence of this. From a negative perspective, believing something that isn't true can have disastrous consequences. It's evident in the thousands of girls whose lives have been ruined through female genital mutilation (FGM) in countries where there is a tradition of female circumcision. Why do they do this? Because they believe that it's the right thing to do! Belief influences behaviour. That's why what we believe is so important.

And as Christians it's the teaching of Jesus that determines what we believe and how we behave. Or at least it should be! We need to believe what he says and put it into practice. In James 2 we're told that believing is not enough. If our faith is genuine it will be expressed in action:

> *What good is it, my brothers, if a man claims to have faith but has no deeds? Can such faith save him? Suppose a brother or sister is without clothes and daily food. If one of you says to him, "Go, I wish you well; keep warm and well fed," but does nothing about his physical needs, what good is it? In the same way, **faith by itself, if it is not accompanied by action, is dead** (vv.14-17).*

So when our faith, our belief in Jesus, is real it will be accompanied by action. If we love him we will do what he says – even when it seems crazy! Let me give you one small example. As a teenager I was personally challenged by what Jesus says in Matthew chapter 5:

> *You have heard that it was said, 'Eye for eye, and tooth for tooth.' But I tell you, Do not resist an evil person. **If someone strikes you on the right cheek, turn to him the other also**...*

*You have heard that it was said, 'Love your neighbour and hate your enemy. 'But I tell you: **Love your enemies** and pray for those who persecute you, that you may be sons of your Father in heaven* (vv.38-39, 43-45).

Did Jesus mean that literally, or was there another explanation? Now explain it away as much as you like, I couldn't escape the clear meaning of what Jesus said. If someone hit me, I was not to hit back. Shortly after coming to this decision, I had an unexpected opportunity to put into practice what I believed.

It was a Sunday evening and I was walking home after church. Two boys about my age were coming in the opposite direction towards me. Suddenly, as they got level with me, one of them, without warning, took a swing at me and hit me on the side of my face! I think I was surprised rather than hurt. I didn't know him. As far as I know, he didn't know me. I hadn't done anything that could have offended him. So why did he hit me? I didn't ask, but, remembering Jesus' teaching, I said, 'I don't know why you did that, but, if it gave you any pleasure, perhaps you'd like to hit the other side now'. How did he react? A look of sheer amazement, an embarrassed laugh, followed by a speedy retreat!

Now let me make it clear. I'm not suggesting that Jesus gave us these instructions as a piece of advice on self-defence! I think that in such circumstances we should expect to be hit a second time, but I believe that on this occasion God was honouring my obedience to the words of the Lord Jesus. And I'm not trying to tell anyone else how they should behave. I'm just asking the question, *How seriously do we take what Jesus says?* John tells us that we love him because he first loved us (1 John 4:19) and Jesus said that if we love him we will do what he says (John 14:15).

What we believe is vitally important because it affects our ultimate destiny.

The most important thing Jesus teaches us is to believe in him. Trusting in Jesus is the only way of salvation. The things we have done wrong separate us from a holy God. Our only means of access to God, either in this life or the next, is through Jesus. That's because only Jesus was good enough to take the punishment our sins deserve. In the words of an old hymn:

> *There was no other good enough to pay the price of sin.*
>
> *He only could unlock the gate of heaven and let us in.*

Nowhere is this clearer than in John's Gospel where Jesus clearly states:

> *I am the way and the truth and the life.* **No one** *comes to the Father except through me* (John 14:6).

Peter proclaims the same truth when, talking about Jesus, he says:

> *Salvation is found in no one else, for there is* **no other name** *under heaven given to men by which we must be saved* (Acts 4:12).

And Paul tells us that

> *there is one God and* **one mediator between God and men,** *the man Christ Jesus who gave himself as a ransom for all* (1 Timothy 2:5-6).

We can't put things right with God by trying to do better or 'turning over a new leaf'. Our only hope is for God to have mercy on us – and he will, if we put our trust in Jesus. What he says in John 3 could not be clearer:

28

16 *"For God so loved the world that he gave his one and only Son, that whoever believes in him shall not perish but have eternal life... Whoever believes in him is not condemned, but whoever does not believe stands condemned already because he has not believed in the name of God's one and only Son...Whoever believes in the Son has eternal life, but whoever rejects the Son will not see life, for God's wrath remains on him* (vv. 16, 18, 36).

What we believe is vitally important because it affects our ultimate destiny.

God speaks to us in the actions of Jesus

In his letter to the Galatians Paul lists nine wonderful qualities which he calls *the fruit of the Spirit[8]*. These qualities should be evident in the life of every Christian as they reflect the character of Jesus which the indwelling Spirit of Christ seeks to reproduce in us. They are *love, joy, peace, patience, kindness, goodness, faithfulness, gentleness, and self-control* (Galatians 5:22-23).

As we read the Gospels it is not difficult to see these qualities in the life of the Lord Jesus. And, as we see what Jesus did, God speaks to us challenging us to do the same. *Our attitude should be the same as that of Christ Jesus* (Philippians 2:5). And, of course, our attitude will determine our actions. Let's look at this wonderful 'fruit' in more detail asking God to speak to us through the attitude and actions of Jesus. We'll take them in reverse order from the list in Galatians so that we will conclude with love which is undeniably the greatest of all the fruit of the Spirit (1 Corinthians 13:13).

---

[8] You'll find similar lists in Colossians 3:12-15 and 1 Corinthians 13:4-8.

Self-control

Right at the start of his ministry, straight after he was baptised in the River Jordan, Jesus was led into the desert by the Spirit to be tempted by the devil. Then, Matthew tells us:

> *After fasting for forty days and forty nights, he was hungry* (Matthew 4:2).

He was hungry. What an understatement! He had eaten nothing for six weeks! I feel hungry if I haven't eaten for six hours! Then, suddenly, an opportunity comes to break his fast. Some of the stones in the desert may have looked like loaves of bread. *You're the Son of God, aren't you?* says Satan, *Why not turn these stones into bread?* Now Jesus knew that he *was* the Son of God. God has said so (just three verses earlier) at his baptism:

> *This is my Son, whom I love; with him I am well pleased* (Matthew 3:17).

Jesus knew that he had the power to do what Satan suggested, but just because you can doesn't mean that you should. I can't imagine how strong the temptation to eat must have been, but Jesus chose to listen to his Father rather than to Satan. He answered:

> *It is written: 'Man does not live on bread alone, but on every word that comes from the mouth of God'* (Matthew 4:4).

What amazing self-control! Where did it come from? His relationship with God, his desire to please him and his knowledge of God's word. Could there be any greater demonstration of self-control? Yes, and we find it in Matthew's account of the crucifixion:

> *Those who passed by hurled insults at him... saying... 'Save yourself. Come down from the cross if you are the Son of God!'* (Matthew 27:39-40).

And Jesus was the Son of God, and he could have come down from the cross. But he didn't. Despite the agony, he stayed there. Why? Because he knew that if we were to be saved he must die for our sins. He must pay the price. He must take the punishment. So he stayed there. He stayed there because he loved us. Let God speak to you through the example of Jesus' self-control.

Humility

The Greek word translated as *gentleness* in Galatians 5:23 carries with it the thought of *humility*. Paul uses it a few verses later when he says:

> *Brothers, if someone is caught in a sin, you who are spiritual should restore him* **gently**. *But watch yourself, or you also may be tempted* (Galatians 6:1).

This warning, to watch yourself because you might be tempted too, clearly implies that Paul is using the word *gently* to mean *in a spirit of humility*. This is confirmed by the paraphrase in the Amplified Bible which interprets *gently* as *not with a sense of superiority or self-righteousness*. So it seems reasonable to assume that this is how he is using it when talking about the fruit of the Spirit just a few verses earlier.

The humility of Jesus is most clearly expressed in two main New Testament passages. The first is **Philippians 2:5-11.**

> *Your attitude should be the same as that of Christ Jesus: Who, being in very nature God, did not consider equality with God*

*something to be grasped, but made himself nothing, taking the very nature of a servant, being made in human likeness. And being found in appearance as a man, he **humbled** himself and became obedient to death – even death on a cross!*

This passage speaks for itself. It took humility for someone who was equal with God to become a man, to become a servant, to become nothing. And yet he humbled himself even further. He became obedient to death, even death on a cross. And as Christians we're encouraged to have the same attitude.

The second passage is **John 13:1-17** where Jesus washes his disciples' feet. In verse 1 we're told that *Jesus knew that the time had come for him to leave this world and go to the Father*. He knew that he was shortly to be crucified. But he also knew that *the Father had put all things under his power and that he had come from God and was returning to God* (v.3).

And so he did something that would be an active demonstration of the truth later to be expressed by Paul in Philippians 2. It would demonstrate his humility and give his disciples an object lesson in how they too should behave. He got up from the meal, took off his outer clothing, and wrapped a towel around his waist (v.4). Then he poured water into a basin and began to wash his disciples' feet, drying them with the towel (v.5).

This was a symbol of what he would accomplish on the cross enabling his disciples to be washed clean by the shedding of his blood. That's why it was important that Peter, who had protested, should allow Jesus to wash his feet too (vv.6-10). And Jesus' humility, his willingness to wash feet, to cleanse us from sin, was another expression of his love.

Finally, when Jesus had finished washing their feet he put on his clothes and returned to his place (v.12)[9]. Then he said:

> *Do you understand what I have done for you? You call me 'Teacher' and 'Lord,' and rightly so, for that is what I am. Now that I, your Lord and Teacher, have washed your feet, you also should wash one another's feet.* **I have set you an example that you should do as I have done for you.** *I tell you the truth, no servant is greater than his master, nor is a messenger greater than the one who sent him. Now that you know these things, you will be blessed if you do them (vv.12-17).*

Let God speak to you through the example of Jesus' humility.

Faithfulness

From the very beginning of his life here on earth Jesus came to do the will of God. Hebrews 10:5-7 tells us that *when Christ came into the world, he said...I have come to do your will, O God.* Even at the age of 12 Jesus knew that God, not Joseph, was his true Father (Luke 2:49). And throughout his life he was faithful to his Father's will. In John 4:34, when the disciples were trying to persuade Jesus to eat something, he said:

> *My food...is to do the will of him who sent me and to finish his work.*

---

[9] What a wonderful symbol of Jesus returning to his place in heaven after he had finished his redemptive work on the cross! Compare Hebrews 1:3 *...After he had provided purification for sins, he sat down at the right hand of the Majesty in heaven.*

And in John 6:38 he says

> *I have come down from heaven not to do my will but to do the will of him who sent me.*

But his faithfulness to God and determination to do his will are no more clearly seen than in the Garden of Gethsamane on the night before Jesus was crucified. In Matthew 26 we're told that he took with him Peter, James and John, and told them, *My soul is overwhelmed with sorrow... Stay here and keep watch with me* (v.38). Jesus then went a little farther and fell with his face to the ground and prayed:

> *My Father, if it is possible, may this cup be taken from me. Yet not as I will, but as you will* (v.39).

He then returns to his disciples and finds them sleeping! And this happens twice more. Jesus prays the same prayer, comes back, and finds them sleeping.

This sad story reveals in stark contrast the unfaithfulness of the disciples and faithfulness of Jesus. The disciples can't even stay awake even at the time of Jesus' greatest need. Jesus knows what's going to happen. The thought of crucifixion horrifies him, and he asks his Father three times if there is any other way. But ultimately, when he knows that there is not, his faithfulness shines through.

> *Yet not as I will, but as you will.*

But this story not only reveals Jesus' faithfulness to God. It shows his faithfulness to his disciples. If Jesus had refused the way of the cross – and he could have – what hope would there have been for them or for us? Perhaps the sight of the disciples sleeping reminded him of the weakness of human nature and our need for him to save us. His faithfulness, motivated by love for his Father and his love for us, gave him the strength to carry on.

Let God speak to you through the example of Jesus' faithfulness.

Goodness and kindness

The English word *goodness*, like the word *good,* can be used in many different ways. It's very flexible. For example, we can talk of a good meal and we can refer to someone as a good person, but the meaning of good in each case is rather different. The same is true of the Greek words for good and goodness (*agathos* and *agathōsunē*). So we can't be entirely sure of how Paul is using the word in Galatians 5:22. However, in the New Testament the word is frequently connected with doing good works and in Colossians 1:10 we read:

> *And we pray this in order that you may live a life worthy of the Lord and may please him in every way: **bearing fruit in every good work**, growing in the knowledge of God,*

The reference to bearing fruit in this verse seems to suggest that the fruit of the Spirit which Paul calls *goodness* relates to:

- Living a life worthy of the Lord

- Pleasing him in every way

- Doing good works

- Growing in the Knowledge of God.

And, of course, that's exactly what Jesus did. He lived a sinless life. He pleased God in every way. As a human being *he grew in wisdom and stature, and in favour with God and man* (Luke 2:52). And Peter, when summarising Jesus' ministry, said of him that *he went about doing good and healing…* (Acts 10:38). He not only **was** good. He **did** good. He was anointed with the Holy Spirit to

> *preach good news to the poor… to proclaim freedom for the prisoners and recovery of sight for the blind, to release the oppressed, to proclaim the year of the Lord's favour* (Luke 4:18-19).

Similarly his *kindness* overflowed again and again as he met the needs of the poor and needy. Consider, for example, his kindness in turning water into wine at the wedding-feast at Cana in Galilee. We are so often preoccupied with the amazing miracle that we neglect the kindness of Jesus in performing it.

And his goodness and kindness were surely motivated by his love. Let God speak to you through the goodness and kindness of Jesus.

Patience

The English word *patience* comes from the Latin verb *patior* meaning *I suffer*. That's why people in hospital are called *patients* – people who are suffering. But the Greek word *makrothumia,* translated as *patience* in Galatians 5:22, has a wider meaning. It comes from two other Greek words, *makros* meaning *far* and *thumos* meaning *wrath* or *anger.* So to exercise *makrothumia* is to keep your anger far from you. It's used elsewhere in the New Testament to mean *patient enduring of evil, slowness of avenging injuries,* or *patient expectation.*

It's not difficult to see all these qualities in the life of the Lord Jesus. He was consistently enduring *opposition from sinners* (Hebrews 12:3), he prayed for the forgiveness of those who crucified him (Luke 23:34) and he *endured the cross, scorning its shame* because he patiently expected *the joy that was set before him* (Hebrews 12:2).

But he was *patient* with his disciples too. They were so slow to learn and to believe. On the eve of his crucifixion they still had not fully understood who he was. In John 14:2-9 Jesus tells them that he is going to prepare a place for them in his Father's house (v.2) and that they know the way (v.4). Thomas says to him:

> Lord, we don't know where you are going, so how can we know the way?

Jesus answers:

> I am the way and the truth and the life. No one comes to the Father except through me. If you really knew me, you would know my Father as well. From now on, you do know him and have seen him (vv.6-7)

Then Philip says:

> Lord, show us the Father and that will be enough for us.

Imagine how Jesus must have felt. In a few hours he's going to be crucified. And still they don't understand who he is. I know personally the frustration of a teacher whose students still haven't got what I've painstakingly tried to teach them! Yet I hear infinite patience in Jesus' reply:

> Don't you know me, Philip, even after I have been among you such a long time? Anyone who has seen me has seen the Father. How can you say, 'Show us the Father'? (v.9).

How amazing! Let God speak to you through the example of Jesus' patience.

Peace and Joy

Peace of heart, as every Christian knows, springs from that peace with God which results from our being in right relationship with him. *Being justified by faith we have peace with God through our Lord Jesus Christ* (Romans 5:1). But Jesus had no need to be justified. He was the sinless one. He always lived in right relationship with Father! Yet there's one occasion when it appears that Jesus is not at peace. As he bears our sins in his body on the cross he cries in anguish:

My God, my God. Why have you forsaken me? (Matt 27:46).

It's as if God has turned his back on his Son. Jesus has forfeited his peace. He's bearing your sin and mine. And God is too holy to look at sin[10]. Jesus sacrifices his peace that we might have peace with God. And he does it because he loves us.

And Jesus' relationship with God was the source of his *joy* too. He lived life in God's presence, and in his presence there is fulness of joy[11]. Luke records that Jesus was *full of joy through the Holy Spirit* (Luke 10:21). What a pity that so many stained-glass windows and paintings portray him with a long and gloomy face! Jesus was a man of joy! Admittedly, he was a man of sorrows and acquainted with grief[12]

But that was primarily at the time of his passion, both in the Garden of Gethsemane and the events that led to his crucifixion. As with his peace, so with his joy. He sacrificed both so that we could have them.

Let God speak to you through the example of Jesus' peace and joy.

---

[10] See Habakkuk 1:13
[11] Psalm 16:11
[12] Isaiah 53:3

Love

Finally, Jesus was a man of *love*. Love is the greatest of the fruit and it is possible to understand Paul's teaching in Galatians as meaning that love *is* the fruit and that the eight other qualities are manifestations of it. That's what I've been trying to demonstrate as we've looked at each of the fruit of the Spirit. They are all, in one way or another, a manifestation of love[13].

Jesus' love is evident throughout the New Testament, not just in the Gospels. Paul could refer to him as the Son of God who *loved* me and gave himself for me (Galatians 2:20) and this reference to the cross reminds us that Calvary is the greatest demonstration of love the world has ever seen. And, what's more, Paul says he did it *for me*.

In this chapter we have seen how God speaks to us through the person, the words, and the actions of Jesus. In all these three ways God continues to speak through Jesus, revealing what God is like, teaching us what to believe, and showing us how we should live. But, most important of all, he is telling us that he loves us.

---

[13] Compare, for example, Colossians 3:12-14

PART TWO

GOD SPEAKS THROUGH THE BIBLE

CHAPTER TWO

Why believe that God speaks to us through the Bible

So far we have seen that God speaks to all people through creation, that in Old Testament times God spoke to Israel through the prophets, and that now God has spoken finally and definitively by his Son, the Lord Jesus Christ. We now turn our attention to another way that God speaks to us. He speaks through his written word, the Bible. In this chapter we will consider *why* we should believe that God speaks to us through the Bible. In the following chapters we'll look at *how* he does so.

So why should we believe that God speaks to us through the Bible? Here are five reasons:

- The Bible shows us the way of salvation
- The Bible tells us about Jesus
- Jesus taught that God speaks through Scripture
- The apostles taught that God speaks through Scripture
- Christian experience confirms that God speaks through the Bible.

The Bible shows us the way of salvation

It's important to believe that God speaks to us through the Bible because it's the Bible that shows us the way of salvation. The Scriptures *are able to make you wise for salvation through faith in Christ Jesus* (2 Timothy 3:15).

Peter tells us that we ... *have been born again, not of perishable seed, but of imperishable, through the living and enduring word of God* (1 Peter 1:23) and Paul tells us that faith for salvation comes from hearing the word of God (Romans 10:17).

If you're like me, your first experience of hearing God speak to you was when he spoke through the preaching of his word challenging you to repent and put your trust in Christ as your Saviour. He spoke to you through the Bible then, and he will continue to do so throughout your Christian life. And closely connected with the fact that the Bible shows us the way od salvation is the fact that it tells us about Jesus.

The Bible tells us about Jesus

We saw in the last chapter that God speaks to us through Jesus, showing us what God is like, teaching us what to believe, and demonstrating through his example how we should live. But how do we *know* all these things about Jesus? Because they are recorded in the *Bible*.

Admittedly, our first acquaintance with the facts about Jesus may not have come directly from the Bible, but from someone telling us about Jesus - maybe our parents, or a Sunday school teacher, a Christian minister, or a friend. But, of course, whoever it was who first told us about Jesus, they first got the information from the Bible.

So God speaks to us through Jesus who is his final word to the human race (Hebrews 1:1), and he speaks to us through the Bible which is his record of who Jesus is, and what he said and did. The Bible is all about Jesus. Even the Old Testament scriptures, written long before he came, are about him:

> *And beginning with Moses and all the Prophets, he (Jesus) explained to them what was said in **all the Scriptures** concerning himself* (Luke 24:27).

So God speaks to us through Jesus and it is through the Bible that he tells us about him.

Jesus taught that God speaks through scripture

Another good reason for believing that God speaks to us through the Bible is that Jesus himself believed this. With regard to the Old Testament, Jesus stated that *the scripture cannot be broken* (John 10:35). The Sadducees were in error because they were ignorant of the scriptures (Mark 12:24). It was *easier for heaven and earth to disappear than for the least stroke of a pen to drop out of the law* (Luke 16:17).

As far as Jesus was concerned, when the Bible spoke, *God* spoke. For example, in Genesis 2:24 the **Bible** says:

> *That is why a man leaves his father and mother and is united to his wife, and they become one flesh.*

But in Matthew 19:4-5 Jesus says:

> *Haven't you read... that at the beginning the Creator... said, "For this reason a man will leave his father and mother and be united to his wife, and the two will become one flesh"?*

So for Jesus, when the Bible speaks, God speaks. It is surely enough for us, as Jesus' disciples, to believe as he believed. The New Testament, of course, had not been written at the time of Christ. But Jesus promised his disciples that the Holy Spirit would accurately remind them of his teachings and would lead them into further truth for which they were not yet ready:

> But the Advocate, the Holy Spirit, whom the Father will send in my name, will **teach you all things** and will **remind you of everything** I have said to you (John 14:26).

> But when he, the Spirit of truth, comes, he will **guide you into all the truth.** ...He will **tell you what is yet to come** (John 16:13).

In later chapters we'll be talking about various ways that God speaks to us by his Spirit. But the primary way the Holy Spirit speaks to us is through the Bible.

The apostles taught that God speaks through scripture

As we read the New Testament we discover that the first Christians believed that God spoke through the scriptures of both the Old and New Testaments. Paul tells us that *all Scripture is God-breathed and is useful for teaching, rebuking, correcting and training in righteousness* (2 Timothy 3:16).

Peter tells us that he and the other apostles did not follow cleverly devised stories when they spoke about Jesus. They were eyewitnesses of his majesty. They heard the voice of God saying, *This is my Son, whom I love; with him I am well pleased.* But he then goes on to say:

> We also have the **prophetic message** as something **completely reliable**, and you will do well to pay attention to it, as to a light shining in a dark place, until the day dawns and the morning star rises in your hearts. Above all, you must

*understand that **no prophecy of Scripture came about by the prophet's own interpretation** of things. For prophecy never had its origin in the human will, but **prophets, though human, spoke from God as they were carried along by the Holy Spirit*** (2 Peter 1:16-21).

This shows us that the Scriptures are completely reliable. The people who wrote them were speaking from God. The writings of the Scriptures are as much the voice of God as the experience Peter had when he heard God's voice in audible form.

What's more, the New Testament writers were aware of the inspiration that Jesus had promised. Their writings were not a product of their own wisdom or ability. They were conscious of direct guidance and authority from God. The things they wrote were *the commandments of the Lord* taught directly by the Holy Spirit (1 Corinthians 2:13, 14:37) and their writings were acknowledged as equal to those of the Old Testament.

Notice how, in 1 Timothy 5:18, Paul quotes the New Testament alongside the Old Testament and evidently considers both as an integral part of scripture:

> *For the scripture says, Do not muzzle the ox while it is treading out the grain* (Deuteronomy 25:4) *and, The worker deserves his wages* (Matthew 10:10).

The same attitude is adopted by Peter in 2 Peter 3:16, where he refers to all Paul's letters as part of the scriptures:

> *He (Paul) writes the same way in **all his letters**, speaking in them of these matters. His letters contain some things that are hard to understand, which ignorant and unstable people*

*distort, as they do **the other Scriptures**, to their own destruction.*

It is clear, then, that both Jesus and his early followers taught that the scriptures are the written word of God and that, therefore, as we read them he will speak to us. The message is simple. If you want God to speak to you, read the Bible!

Christian experience confirms that God speaks through the Bible

I'm sure that countless millions of Christians can testify that God has spoken to them through the Bible. It may have been through reading the Bible, or someone else preaching from it, or through a verse of Scripture that has suddenly come to mind just when it was needed. Perhaps, like me, you've heard God speak to you in all of these ways. As we've just seen with regard to Peter's experience, the writings of the Scriptures are as much God's voice as when he heard it in audible form. But let me give you just one example from my personal experience of how God spoke to me and through me from two Bible passages in a very unusual situation.

Some years ago I was invited by the Christian Union of a college in Chester to conduct an evangelistic mission among the students. When I arrived just after lunch on the Monday, a member of staff conducted me to the bedroom they had allocated for me.

> *I hope you don't mind*, he said, *we're putting you in a room that was occupied until recently by a student we have had to expel from the college. He had been practising witchcraft.*

I was rather surprised by this, to say the least, but I put a brave face on it and said, as casually as I could, *Oh, that's fine. No problem!* But when I entered the room, I confess I began to wonder what evil presence might be lurking there. The half-burnt candle on the windowsill didn't help. Had that been part of his devilish paraphernalia? Or had they just had a power-cut recently?

Then I remembered what Jesus had promised to his disciples as he sent them out on the task of world evangelisation:

> *Surely, I will be with you always, to the very end of the age* (Matthew 28:20).

I reminded myself of other Bible verses like

> *Behold I give you power over all the power of the enemy, and nothing shall by any means hurt you* (Luke 10:19)

and I began to take courage. I settled into my room and started to prepare myself for the meeting at which I had to speak that evening.

After a few minutes there was a knock at the door. Two men stood there. They had seen the light on in my room and wondered who it was that was in there.

> *Are you a new student?* they asked.

> *No,* I replied, *I've come to conduct a mission for the Christian Union.*

> *That's interesting,* said one of them. *It's strange they should put you in my old room.*

It was the man they had expelled for practising witchcraft! He had come back to visit his friend. Of course, I invited them to the meeting that evening and the 'witch' said he might come. And sure enough, when the time for the meeting came, there he was sitting in the audience.

I preached the gospel and I would like to be able to say that the man gave his life to Christ, but he didn't. Instead, he came and argued with me! This went on for some time after the meeting had closed, and after about half an hour, feeling that we were getting nowhere by arguing, I decided to invite him to come to the meeting the next day.

> *I think you'll be particularly interested tomorrow, I said. The subject is Jesus the way to power. How real is the supernatural? Is it safe?*

> *I don't think you know the first thing about the supernatural,* he replied.

What a challenge to a Pentecostal preacher!

> *Well, I don't know much about what you get up to when you practise your witchcraft, I said, but I will tell you one thing. When you come under the control of a familiar spirit, you can't say Jesus is Lord, can you?*

I don't know who was more surprised, him or me! I had said this on the basis of my understanding of 1 Corinthians 12:1-3, but I was not prepared for the effect it had on this young man. He went visibly pale and said,

> *How did you know that?*

Taking courage by his reaction, I said:

Because the Bible, which is God's word tells me so. And I'll tell you something else it says. You may not acknowledge that Jesus is Lord now, but the day is coming when you will have to, whether you like it or not. For the Bible says that one day at the name of Jesus every knee shall bow, of things in heaven and things on earth and things under the earth, and every tongue confess that Jesus Christ is Lord to the glory of God the Father

As I quoted these verses from Philippians 2:10-11 to him, he retreated out of the room! I went to bed at around 11pm and fell asleep straight away, sleeping soundly until about 7 the next morning. While the students were having their breakfast, I went down the corridor to the washroom to shave. While I was shaving, I saw in the mirror the face of the 'witch'. He was standing right behind me.

Good morning, he said. *Did you sleep well?*

Yes, thank you, I replied.

Are you sure?

Yes, perfectly sure. I went to bed around 11 and slept soundly until about 7.

Really? I can't understand that!

Why? What's so unusual about having a good night's sleep?

Well, you see, he confessed, *I was so annoyed with what you said last night that I stayed up all night practising my witchcraft. I was trying to get a poltergeist into your room to disturb you. I've done it many times before and it's never*

51

failed. That's why they expelled me from the college. I can't understand why it didn't work this time.

Oh, I said, *I wish you had told me. I could have told you not to waste your time. Don't you know that Christians are immune to such things?*

Later that day he was seen leaving the college with his bag packed.

Leaving? said one of the Christians. *Aren't you coming to the meeting today?*

No, he replied, *that fellow knows too much about the supernatural.*

Now how does all that relate to God speaking to us through the Bible? Please notice five things:

- The Bible passages I quoted were passages I had memorised.
- They came into my mind as the Holy Spirit reminded me of them.
- They were directly relevant to the situation.
- They brought glory to Jesus.
- They had a powerful effect on an unbeliever.

The word of God is powerful and the Holy Spirit who inspired it can use it to speak to us and through us as we allow him to. Christian experience really does confirm that God speaks through the Bible to Christians and non-Christians too.

CHAPTER THREE

Understanding the Bible correctly

In the last chapter we considered *why* we should believe that God speaks to us through the Bible. In the next few chapters will be looking at *how* he does so. But first it will be important to consider how to understand the Bible correctly.

We have already seen that as far as Jesus was concerned, when the Bible spoke, *God* spoke[14]. We also said that the writings of the Scriptures are as much the voice of God as the experience Peter had when he heard God's voice in audible form on the Mount of Transfiguration[15]. All that's true, but it clearly needs further explanation.

We know from the account of when Jesus was tempted in the desert that the devil can quote Scripture[16]. The Scripture he quoted from Psalm 91 is certainly the word of God, but Satan was misapplying it, and Jesus knew it! From this we learn the importance of correctly understanding what the Bible is saying, and in this chapter I'll be outlining some of the things we need to bear in mind when asking what God might be saying to us through a particular verse or passage. Before we jump to a conclusion as to what it means, there are two basic questions we need to ask:

- *What part of the Bible are we reading?*

- *What is the context of the passage we are reading?*

---

[14] See page 45

[15] Pages 46-47

[16] Matthew 4:6

What part of the Bible are we reading?

The first thing we need to be aware of is whether the passage we're reading is from the Old Testament or the New. Whenever we read the OT it is important to remember that it is not God's final revelation to the human race. As the writer to the Hebrews pointed out:

> In the past God spoke to our ancestors through the prophets at many times and in various ways, but in these last days he has spoken to us by his Son, whom he appointed heir of all things, and through whom also he made the universe
> (Hebrews 1:1-2).

We need to understand that Jesus himself is the fulfilment of all OT law and prophecy:

> Do not think that I have come to abolish the Law or the Prophets; I have not come to abolish them but to fulfil them
> (Matthew 5:17).

The OT is a revelation of the old covenant that God made with his people, but the OT itself promised that the day would come when God would make a new and better covenant with them. This is made very clear in the letter to the Hebrews. As Christians, we are not living under the old covenant that God made with the Jewish people, but under the new covenant which is sealed with the blood of Jesus. John 19:30 tells us that when Jesus died on the cross he declared, IT IS FINISHED. The word 'finished' here means 'accomplished' or 'completed'. Jesus had completed the work his Father had given him to do. His death on the cross provided atonement for our sins and was the fulfilment of all OT law. This is why we should always read the OT in the light of the NT. A good example of how to apply this practice is the OT food laws.

The Old Testament food laws as an example

We'll use Leviticus 11:1-8 as a passage that represents the sort of things the Israelites were allowed to eat and not to eat. Camels, hyraxes, rabbits and pigs were forbidden, but an animal that both chews the cud and has a divided hoof was permitted.

We don't need to concern ourselves with *why* the Lord gave Moses these instructions. What is significant is that the instructions were given to *the Israelites*. But how do we know that they don't apply to us as well? To answer this we need to consider various passages in the New Testament.

First, notice what Jesus said in Mark 7:14-23. He makes it clear that nothing outside a person can defile them by going into them because it doesn't go into their heart but into their stomach, and then out of the body. Mark then clarifies this by saying:

> *In saying this, Jesus declared **all foods clean**.*

This certainly seems to mean that for us as Christians there's no such thing as unclean food. But how does this stand up in the light of Acts 15:22-29? In this passage we have a record of a decision made by the early church in order to resolve a particular problem they were facing at the time. Some of the Jewish believers, because of their Old Testament background, had been teaching that Gentiles who became Christians should be circumcised in line with OT teaching. This was clearly causing great difficulty for the Gentile converts and a meeting of the apostles and elders was called to resolve the problem.

The decision they came to, with the help of the Holy Spirit, was that the Gentile converts did not need to be circumcised - something which Paul makes very clear in his letter to the Galatians - but that there were certain things that the Gentiles should abstain from. So they sent them a letter saying:

> *It seemed good to the Holy Spirit and to us not to burden you with anything beyond the following requirements:* **You are to abstain from food sacrificed to idols, from blood, from the meat of strangled animals and from sexual immorality.**

But does this mean that those prohibitions apply to Christians today? In my opinion, with the exception of the last item in the list, which is of course forbidden in the rest of the NT, the answer is no. I say this for three reasons:

1. Acts 15 is a record of a decision made by the church at a specific time to resolve a problem that was current at that point in history. It is not necessary to understand it as being applicable to Christians today who are living in quite different circumstances.
2. The decision was almost certainly made so that the Jewish Christians would not be unnecessarily offended. This interpretation is certainly in line with Paul's teaching in Romans 14 and 1 Corinthians 10[17].
3. It is very clear from Paul's epistles that Christians are not subject to legalistic regulations, but that out of love for our fellow believers we should modify our behaviour so as not to cause anyone to stumble.

---

[17] Romans 14:1-21, 1 Corinthians 10:23-33, cf. 1 Timothy 4:45.

In short, Paul clearly teaches that it doesn't matter what we eat or drink as long as we can do it with a clear conscience and will not distress someone else by doing so. The underlying consideration is LOVE. The whole law is summarised in this:

> For the entire law is fulfilled in keeping this one command: 'Love your neighbour as yourself.' (Galatians 5:14).

> Jesus replied: '"Love the Lord your God with all your heart and with all your soul and with all your mind." This is the first and greatest commandment. And the second is like it: "Love your neighbour as yourself." All the Law and the Prophets hang on these two commandments'" (Matthew 22:37-40).

In this example with regard to the OT food laws, which we've used to illustrate how the Old Testament must be interpreted in the light of the New, we've been careful not to read a passage in isolation, but to compare scripture with scripture. We have also touched on another important principle with regard to how to interpret the Bible correctly – the context of the book or passage we are reading.

What is the context of the passage?

The question of context is undoubtedly the most important issue with regard to understanding correctly what God is saying. We've already dealt with the most basic aspect – *Which part of the Bible are you looking at? OT or NT?* But there are three other areas in which context is vitally important:

- The literary context
- The cultural/historical context
- The immediate context.

The literary context

The Bible is not really a book. It's a collection of books. In the Greek New Testament the word for bible is plural and it means *the books*. These books were written over a period of some 1500 years by a wide range of people in many different places. If we want to understand a book correctly we need to consider its *genre* – what kind of literature it is. Here's a brief summary of the different kinds of literature we find in the Bible:

Types of OT literature

- Narrative (found mainly from Genesis to Esther)

- The Law (found in the Pentateuch, the first five books)

- The Psalms

- Wisdom (Proverbs, Job, Ecclesiastes, Song of Songs)

- The Prophets

Types of NT Literature

- Narrative (The Gospels, Acts)

- Parables (found mainly in the Gospels)

- Letters

- Apocalyptic (Revelation).

The reason it's helpful to know what type of literature we are reading is that, although all Scripture is inspired by God[18], the way he may speak to us through it may vary according to the kind of literature it is. For example, in the narrative passages we may learn from the

---

[18] 2 Timothy 3:16

example of what happened to God's people in the past[19], but in the NT letters we're given direct instructions as to what to do. We learn from all these different kinds of literature, but we learn in different ways. To use the illustration of the OT food laws again, you will have noticed that I based my conclusions on what Paul said in his letters rather than on the narrative of what the early church decided in the book of Acts. I was taking the *genre*, the literary context, into consideration.

The cultural/historical context

Although the books of the Bible were inspired by the Holy Spirit, God used human authors to write them. The epistles, for example, are conditioned by the language and culture of the first century. They speak to specific situations in the first century church. Their authors lived at a certain point in history and in a society where the culture was often very different from ours today.

This is reflected in their writings and if we understand their culture we will understand more clearly what God might be saying through them. And although some passages may not seem directly relevant to us today, we should be able to see the principles being taught in them and apply them to situations that arise in our own lives and the life of the church today.

One example of this might be how we understand Paul's teaching on eating food that has been offered to idols. The Christians in Corinth were confronted with this problem on a daily basis[20], and there are parts of the world where Paul's teaching is still highly relevant today.

---

[19] 1 Corinthians 10:6, for example

[20] For an excellent explanation of Paul's teaching in 1 Corinthians 8-10, see Fee, Gordon D., *The First Epistle to the Corinthians*, Grand Rapids, Eerdmans, 1987.

However, if you're like me, this may not be an issue that has ever arisen for you personally. But does this mean that those of us who have never been in those circumstances can learn nothing from what Paul says on the subject in 1 Corinthians 8?

By no means! The *principles* Paul teaches will always be relevant wherever we live and whatever the culture may be. However much we may think we know, our first duty is to love other people (vv. 1-3). We must be careful that our freedom in Christ does not become a stumbling-block to those who are weak (v.9). It's better not to exercise our freedom if it's going to cause a brother or sister to fall into sin (v.13). So even if we're not in a situation where we're likely to be invited to meat that's been sacrificed to an idol, it's not difficult to think of ways in which we can apply the principles Paul teaches in this chapter. For example, although the New Testament nowhere teaches total abstinence from alcohol, many Christians feel that they should abstain rather than setting an example that might lead others into addiction.

So, to summarise what we've said so far in this chapter, when we're reading a particular passage or verse and we want to understand what God is saying to us through it, we need to be aware of what part of the Bible we are reading – Old or New Testament. We should also bear in mind the literary context and the historical and cultural context in which it was written.

If you're not sure about this, there are many different sources that will help you. The Bible you are reading may already have the information available. The NIV Life Application Bible, for example, at the beginning of each individual book of the Bible, gives you a useful summary of what the book is about, and provides a basic outline of the context it in which it was written. With all that in mind, you're now in a position to consider the immediate context.

The immediate context

By *the immediate context* I mean the verses and chapters around the verse or passage you're looking at. The key to the meaning of a verse will usually be found in the verses that precede it and those that follow it. Take, for example, the last two sentences I have written. In the first sentence I used the word *around*. Now *around* can have a variety of meanings depending on the context in which it's being used. If you don't believe me, take a look in a dictionary! One I just consulted listed at least eight different meanings[21]. But I wasn't using the word to mean *all* these things. The key to how I was using it is found in the second sentence. I used *around* to mean *the verses that precede and those that follow* the verse or passage we're studying.

So be careful! Don't read into a word every possible meaning it can have. Sadly, far too often have I heard preachers fall into this error. The Greek, they tell us, can mean this, or this, or that. That may well be true, but it almost certainly can't be meaning all those things in one particular verse. Let me illustrate this further with the use of two examples, one from modern English and one from NT Greek.

First, let's think about the English word *court*. As a noun it can refer to a law court (the building or the people assembled within it), or a tennis court, or a courtyard. As a verb it can be used in expressions like to court someone's favour, or to mean to be dating someone. Now let's imagine that some zealous Bible student decides to check out the origin of this word and he discovers that *court* (English) comes from the French word *cour* which basically means an enclosed

---

[21] About, round, by, near, next to, alive, existent, living.

space. This comes from the Latin word *hortus* and the Greek word *chortos*, both of which mean *garden*. And if he studies further our student will discover that all the various meanings of our English word *court* are historically connected with the original concept of an enclosed space.

But, as interesting as all this might be – and as a linguist I have always been fascinated by the meaning and origin of words – it is of little value in helping us to understand the meaning of the word *court* in a particular English sentence. The **context** will usually make it abundantly plain.

The same applies to the origin of the Greek word *sōzō* which basically means *to make safe.* Long before the New Testament documents came to be written, *sōzō* was being used in a wide variety of ways, rather like the way we use the English word *save* today. We can talk about saving money, or saving time, or saving a goal in football, or saving someone from drowning, or being saved from our sins.

In the Greek language spoken at the time of the New Testament, sōzō was used in all of these ways – with the obvious exception of football! Its basic meaning is *make safe* or *deliver from a direct threat* or *bring safe and sound out of a difficult situation.*

So it is not surprising to discover that New Testament writers use sōzō in a variety of different contexts, rather like we use save in many different ways today. They apply it mainly in three quite distinct and different contexts, salvation from sin, deliverance from disease, and rescue from danger.

So it can mean *save* or *heal* or *rescue*. But it won't mean all of these things at the same time! When Peter is walking on water and begins to sink, he cries, *Lord, save me!* He doesn't mean *heal me* and he doesn't mean *save me from my sins*. He means *rescue me*. The immediate context makes it plain.

One way to avoid this pitfall is to read the passage in two or three different translations comparing them with each other. Although I have numerous hard copies of different Bible translations, I rarely use them today as it's so easy now to access them online[22].

And although I have been studying Greek for over seventy years – and have taught it to several generations of Bible College students – and have found it of great value in my study of the New Testament, I would strongly recommend that, for most Christians, the use of the many various English translations that are available to us is more than enough to help us understand what God is saying to us through his word.

So I suggest that you read a passage two or three times using a different translation or version each time. As you do so, begin to ask yourself questions. The questions will vary depending on the passage you're reading, but the following should be a helpful guide.

Who said it? To whom?

These are obviously very important questions to ask. For example, the Bible records not only the words of God, but also the words of men. It also on rare occasions records the words of Satan. We have examples of all three in the book of Job. Of course, it's clear when it's Satan who's speaking because the Bible tells us so and we aren't in any danger in confusing what Satan says with the voice of God. But it's not always so straightforward when it comes to what men are saying. Much of the book is a record of the very bad advice Job's so-

---

[22] I find YouVersion very helpful with this

called comforters were giving him, so to ask the question Who said it? is clearly very important. We mustn't receive the advice of Job's friends as if it were God speaking to us.

And it's equally important to ask who the verse or passage is being written or spoken to. As we've already said, what God said to Israel in the Old Testament is not necessarily what he's saying to us as Christians today. Indeed, the New Testament teaches very clearly that it is not. I will say more about this when we talk about God's promises in the next chapter, but to illustrate the point, God's promise to Abraham that he would become the father of a great nation was clearly specific to Abraham and is not directly applicable to us today. So as we read the Bible it's always important to ask who said it or wrote it and to whom it is being said.

Why? In what circumstances?
Another question that it might be helpful to ask is why and in what circumstances the writer has said what we're reading. Sometimes it's perfectly obvious, but if we're not sure, a look at the immediate context will help us. For example, what did Peter mean when he said, *By his wounds you have been healed* (1 Peter 2:24)?

Some Christians believe that this means that because Jesus died for us we can claim healing from all our sicknesses, but a look at the context in which Peter said it suggests that this is not what he meant. The next verse makes it clear that Peter is referring to healing from the wounds of sin. And if you read the preceding verses you will see that Peter is talking to slaves who were often unjustly punished, and Peter is encouraging them to follow the example of Jesus who, though he was completely innocent, *bore our sins in his body on the tree so that we might die to sins and live for righteousness.*

So by considering the context and the circumstances in which Peter is writing we see that there is no mention of the healing of our sicknesses, either in the immediate context or anywhere else in the rest of the letter for that matter[23]. In fact the overall purpose of the letter is to encourage Christians who are being persecuted to endure suffering rather than to escape from it. But that brings us to the next question that it's useful to ask.

What is the main theme of the passage?

Now, assuming that you've done as I've suggested and read through the passage two or three times, preferably using different versions of the Bible, you should be getting a fairly clear idea of the writer's main theme or purpose. One thing that will help you to do this might be to ask if there are any key words that are repeated in the passage. In the section of 1 Peter we've been looking at you will notice the repetition of words like *suffer* and *submit*. As we've just seen, the main purpose of 1 Peter is to encourage Christians who are suffering persecution. And if we look at the immediate context of 1 Peter 2:24 we see that it's set in a section where Peter is teaching his readers the importance of submitting to authority even if it involved suffering.

Verses 13-17 encourage Christians in general to submit to *every authority* (v13). Verses 18-25 encourage slaves to submit to their masters, and the first six verses of chapter 3 encourage wives to be submissive to their husbands. The purpose of this submission is that by following the example of Christ (v.21) those who are not yet Christians might be won over (3:1) to Christ and themselves live lives that will glorify God (2:12). So our understanding of this section of 1 Peter and our interpretation of individual verses within it should be

---

[23] For more detailed discussion on this passage, see *Just a Taste of Heaven,* Chapter Eleven

influenced by our knowledge that the main theme of the passage is submission to authority.

Metaphorical or literal?

Another important key to understanding what God is saying to us through the Bible is being aware of the frequent use of metaphor. It's important not to take something literally when the writer is speaking metaphorically. For example, sin is often referred to in terms of sickness. In Isaiah 1, where God is complaining about the sins of Israel he says:

> Ah, sinful nation, a people loaded with guilt, a brood of evildoers, children given to corruption! They have forsaken the LORD; they have spurned the Holy One of Israel and turned their backs on him.
>
> Why should you be beaten anymore? Why do you persist in rebellion? Your whole head is injured, your whole heart afflicted.
>
> From the sole of your foot to the top of your head there is no soundness – only wounds and welts and open sores, not cleansed or bandaged or soothed with oil (Isaiah 1:4-6).

The language used here is clearly metaphorical. In saying that the whole nation is sick, God is not saying that everybody is physically ill. Because of its rebellion and sin it is spiritually sick. Jesus himself uses the same metaphor for sin. When criticised for eating with sinners, he says:

> It is not the healthy who need a doctor, but the sick. I have not come to call the righteous, but sinners (Mark 2:17).

And, as we have already seen, when we read in 1 Peter 2:24 that by his wounds you have been healed the context strongly indicates that Peter is using the quote from Isaiah metaphorically.

So, to summarise what we've been saying in this chapter, if we want to understand correctly what God is saying to us in the Bible, there are several questions that it will be helpful to ask:

- What part of the Bible are we reading? Old or New Testament?
- What is the literary context of the passage we are reading?
- What is the historical and cultural context?
- What is the immediate context?

And in this connection we should ask:

- Who said it and to whom?
- Why and in what circumstances?
- What's the main theme? Are there any key words?
- Whether what's being said is metaphorical or literal?

And finally, and perhaps most important of all, when we've discovered what God is saying in the passage we've been reading, we should ask ourselves:

How does this apply to me?

In the next three chapters we are going to look at some of the ways God speaks to us through the Bible. We'll be considering promises, instructions, and directions.

CHAPTER FOUR

Promises

One of the ways God speaks to us through the Bible is by the many wonderful promises he has made. We read in 2 Peter 1:3-4 that

> *God's divine power has given us everything we need for life and godliness through our knowledge of him who called us by his own glory and goodness.*

> *Through these he has given us his very great and precious **promises**, so that through them you may participate in the divine nature and escape the corruption in the world caused by evil desires.*

And notice the repetition of the word *promise* in the following verses in Hebrews 11:

> *9. By faith Abraham went to live in the land of **promise**, as in a foreign land, living in tents with Isaac and Jacob, heirs with him of the same **promise**.*

> *11. By faith Sarah herself received power to conceive, even when she was past the age, since she considered him faithful who had **promised**.*

> *13. These all died in faith, not having received the things **promised** but having seen them and greeted them from afar...*

> *17. By faith Abraham, when he was tested, offered up Isaac, and he who had received the **promises** was in the act of offering up his only son...*

*33. ...who through faith conquered kingdoms, enforced justice, obtained **promises**, stopped the mounds of lions...*

*39. And all these, though commended through their faith, did not receive what was **promised**...*

But what exactly are these promises? In this chapter we'll look at:

- How to identify God's promises

- How to understand God's promises

- How to receive them

How to identify God's promises

Let's begin by considering the basic meaning of our English word promise. The Oxford English Dictionary defines it as follows:

1. A declaration made to another person with respect to the future, stating that one will do, or refrain from, some specific act, or that one will give some specified thing.

2. Divine assurance of good or blessing.

Notice that the first part of the definition relates to the future. When we make a promise we're saying what we will or won't do in the future. Statements about what we have or haven't done in the past, although sometimes referred to as promises, are probably better understood as solemn assurances. I can't promise you that I did something yesterday. If I say, 'I promise you I did...' I really mean 'I assure you that I did...'.

And that's where the second part of the definition fits in. God's promises are his assurance of his blessing. God is eternal and his assurances of blessing relate not only to the future but to the past and present as well. Consider the following:

A. Do not steal

B. Love one another

C. Christ died for our sins

D. The blood of Christ cleanses us from all sin

E. God is love

F. I will come again

A and B are commands. They are not promises. C, D, E and F are statements. C is a statement about the past. D is a statement about the present. E is a statement about the eternal nature of God. But, if we limit our understanding to the first part of the dictionary definition, only F is a promise because it's a statement about the future.

However, the second part of the dictionary definition defines promise as divine assurance of good or blessing, and according to that definition C, D, E and F are all promises. We can trust confidently in them because they are statements God has made that assure us of his blessing. And we can be sure about them because of God's integrity and his ability. And it is through them that we have become partakers of his divine nature (2 Peter 1:4).

So, although it would be wrong to think that every verse in the Bible is a promise – some are commands, some are questions etc. – we can be sure that, wherever God assures us of his blessing, that is truly a promise he has made.

How to understand God's promises

Once we've identified something as a promise that God has made it's important to make sure that we understand it correctly. We need to look at the context and see who the promise was originally made to. We need to ask what it meant at the time it was made and how, if at all, it applies to us today.

The guidelines we gave in Chapter Three on how to understand the Bible correctly apply as much to God's promises as to everything else in the Bible. So, please, don't just lay hold of a Bible verse and claim it as yours just because you like it, or because it makes you feel good. Make sure that you're understanding it correctly. But that brings us to the important question as to how the early Christians understood the word promise.

So far we've been looking at the way the English dictionary defines the word promise. But, of course, the New Testament was not originally written in English. It was written in Greek. The Greek word for promise is epaggelia (pronounced epangelia). And if we're to fully understand the significance of this word and how to apply it to our lives today we need to look at how it is used in the New Testament.

A detailed examination will not be possible within the scope of this book but in a series of podcasts I made in 2021 I showed how NT writers use the word promise to refer to major themes that relate to our salvation[24] rather than to individual Bible verses. These include:

> *righteousness, sonship, the gift of the Holy Spirit, the promise of an inheritance, victory over death, eternal life, and the promise of Christ coming.*

---

[24]Details from www.davidpetts.org. Also please see *Problems with Claiming God's Promises* in my book *Just a Taste of Heaven.*

It's by reading the Bible and understanding and trusting these promises that we grow in our faith in the Lord Jesus Christ. These are the promises that Paul is referring to when he says:

> *For no matter how many promises God has made, they are "Yes" in Christ* (2 Corinthians 1:20).

This does not mean that we can claim any and every promise in the Bible, as some Christians mistakenly believe. It means that all God's promises – those that relate to our salvation – find their fulfilment in him. Christ IS the fulfilment of all God's promises. There's a sense in which, if you have Christ, you don't need the promises, because you already have them in him! You don't need to 'claim' them! All you have to do is trust them! But that's the subject of the next section.

How to receive God's promises

Claiming God's promises is common terminology in Christian circles today. So why do I say that we don't need to claim them? The first reason is that **nowhere in the New Testament do we find the word** *claim*. Writers use a variety of verbs in connection with *promise* – have, receive, obtain, for example – but never the word *claim*.

As we've already noted, God's promises were seen as already fulfilled in Christ. Some of them we already have, so there's no need to claim them. Others will not yet reach their ultimate fulfilment until the return of Christ. These we have to wait for patiently knowing that our present experience of the Holy Spirit is God's *guarantee* that all will be fulfilled in the age to come. So there is no biblical basis for saying that God's promises are to be claimed.

My second reason is the **faithfulness of God**. The writer to the Hebrews particularly stresses that God's promises are reliable.

Christians are to hold unswervingly to the hope they profess, for *he who promised is faithful* (10:23, cf. 11:11). The Christian's hope is *firm and secure* (6:19), *an anchor for the soul* because God's purpose is *unchanging* (6:17).

Other New Testament verses also stress God's faithfulness and the reliability of his promises. Surely in the light of this the appropriate response to a promise from one who is totally reliable is a simple and implicit trust that he will do what he has said, not an insistence on one's rights on the grounds that he has said it! Such an insistence takes no account of the patience we have already mentioned.

My third reason is the **fatherhood of God**. God's promises are fulfilled in the salvation we receive in Christ. In him we have been brought into right relationship with God, our heavenly Father. Let me give you a personal illustration. I enjoyed throughout my life a very warm and close relationship with my earthly father while he was alive. I knew from him nothing but love, even if in my younger days that love was sometimes tempered with discipline. I count myself privileged to be his son and, because he was the kind of father he was, I not only loved him but I trusted him and respected him.

Such was my relationship with him that I knew that, if he had promised me something which was in his power to do, he would certainly have done it. To claim such a promise — by saying, 'Father, I insist that you give me what you have promised me. Give it to me now. I demand it as my right. You have promised' – would have been to doubt his love, impugn his integrity and question his faithfulness. But because I trusted him and respected him I would not have dreamed of talking to him like that!

So, if I'm not going to claim God's promises, how do I receive them?

First of all, **remember that in Christ all God's salvation promises are already yours.** You are already righteous in God's sight because you have put your trust in Christ (Romans 5:1). You are already a child of God enjoying all the privileges of sonship (John 1:12-14, Romans 8:14-17). God's Spirit already lives within you (Romans 8:9). You already have eternal life (John 3:16) and the promise of an eternal inheritance (2 Peter 1:4-5). All these blessings are described as promises in the New Testament and they are already yours. You don't need to claim them. You don't even need to receive them! They're already yours because you're in Christ.

But what about other promises that don't come into this category? How do I know if they apply to me? Here are some simple guidelines. First, **if the promise applies to all people, it applies to you.** A good example of this would be promises that begin with words like *whoever* or *everyone who*. When God says:

> *Whoever (or everyone who) calls on the name of the Lord will be saved* (Joel 2:32)

the promise clearly applies to everyone and that includes you! A New Testament example of this would be John 3:16.

> *For God so loved **the world** that he gave his one and only Son, that **whoever** believes in him shall not perish but have eternal life.*

Secondly, **if the promise applies to all Christians, it applies to you.** The promise in John 3:16 applies to all humankind. But there are some promises that only apply to Christians. For example, when Jesus promised his disciples, *I am with you always, to the very end of the age* (Matthew 28:20), the promise was clearly intended for all his disciples for all time. But the promise of his presence was not made to those who are not Christians. But if we're Christians this is a promise which we have no need to claim or receive. We simply need to **believe** it.

The fact that some promises are only made to Christians shows that **some of God's promises have conditions attached.** If you're not yet a Christian, the promise of John 3:16 applies to you, because it applies to all. The condition for receiving it is putting your trust in the Lord Jesus Christ. And if you are a Christian, many of God's promises to you are conditional.

For example, the promise in 1 John1:9 that God *will forgive us our sins and cleanse us from all unrighteousness* only applies *if we confess our sins.* So when you're looking at any of the promises God has made, it's important to make sure that you fulfilled any conditions that may be attached.

Finally, let's consider the category of **promises that God made to individuals or to the nation of Israel.** How do they apply to us as Christians? We'll use two examples as illustrations. First, as I mentioned in an earlier chapter, God's promise to Abraham that he would become the father of a great nation (e.g. Genesis 12:2-3) was clearly specific to Abraham. It's not a promise to you or me.

But that does not mean that God cannot speak to us through it. As we read on in Genesis, and indeed in the rest of the Bible, we learn how God graciously fulfilled that promise in a wonderful way. We learn that God is faithful to his promises and are encouraged to believe that he will keep the promises he has made to us.

Secondly, let's consider a promise that has become very popular among Christians in recent years. In Jeremiah 29:11 God says:

I know the plans I have for you... plans to prosper you and not to harm you, plans to give you hope and a future.

This is clearly a promise that is of great encouragement to us as Christians and yet, as we look at the context, it was not made to Christians, but to God's people who were in exile in Babylon in the sixth century before Christ. So how is it of any value to us as Christians today? Quite simply because it very wonderfully summarises truths which we know from elsewhere in Scripture are most definitely applicable to us as Christians.

So, although the promise was not made to us, we know that it is as true for us as it was for those to whom it was first made. And the same is true of many other Bible promises. They reveal the character of God and it is not difficult for us to believe that what he said to his people back then he is still saying to us today.

In conclusion, then, the Bible records many things that God has said. Some of them are statements of fact, some are questions, some are commands, and some are promises. It's important that we distinguish between them. Then, when we have identified a promise, we need to take note of who the promise was made to. As we have seen, not all God's promises are directly applicable to us, although God may very well speak to us through them.

However, some of God's promises – those that I referred to earlier as salvation promises – are most definitely for all who have trusted Christ as Saviour. Some of these are already ours. Others, like the promise of Christ's return and the blessings that accompany it, though guaranteed, are something for which we must patiently wait. It is through faith and patience that we receive God's promises (Hebrews 6:12).

Sometimes we may need to take a step of faith and act upon the promise he has made. At other times all we can do is trust him. If God has made a promise, he certainly will keep it. But the timing is in his hands and it's enough for us to know that he loves us, that he knows what is best for us, and that he is always working all things together for our good, because we are called according to his purpose (Romans 8:28).

But in the Bible promises are by no means the only way God speaks to us. He gives us instructions as well. And that will be the subject of the next chapter.

CHAPTER FIVE

Instructions

There are two main ways that God gives us instructions in the Bible:

- He tells us what to believe and how to behave

- He teaches us through the lives of God's people

He shows us what to believe and how to behave

In Chapter One we talked about how God speaks to us in the person, the words, and the actions of Jesus. In the person of Jesus, he reveals the true nature of God. In the words of Jesus, he tells us what we should do. And in the actions of Jesus, we have an example of how we should behave.

This, I believe, is the primary way that God speaks to us through the Bible. It's through the person, the words and the actions of Jesus. These are of course mainly revealed in the four Gospels, but actually, in one way or another, the whole Bible is about Jesus. We're told in 2 Timothy 3:16-17 that

> ***All Scripture*** *is God-breathed and is useful for teaching, rebuking, correcting and training in righteousness, so that the man of God may be thoroughly equipped for every good work.*

And in Luke 24:27 we're told that on the road to Emmaus Jesus explained to two of his disciples *what was said in **all the Scriptures** the things concerning himself.* As he did so we're told that the disciples' hearts *burned within them.* This is something we can all experience as we read or listen to God's word. The Holy Spirit makes a verse or passage come alive to us and we feel an inner excitement as we see how it fits so relevantly into our present situation. But I'll be saying more about this in the next chapter when we talk about how God brings key verses to our attention just as we need them.

So God can speak to us through any part of the Bible and reveal to us more about himself and about his purpose for our lives[25]. This is particularly true of the teaching we find in the NT epistles where the apostle Paul encourages us to acknowledge that the things he wrote are *the commandments of the Lord* (1 Corinthians 14:37).

The epistles were letters written to churches and individuals by apostles like Paul, Peter, James, John, and Jude in the decades that followed the death and resurrection of the Lord Jesus. They contain vital teaching on the major doctrines of the Christian faith and on how we should conduct our lives as God's holy people living in an evil world. As we read them, bearing in mind what we said about *genre* in Chapter Three, we should ask the Lord to show us how to apply their teaching to our lives today. But that leads us to another important way God speaks to us through the Bible.

He teaches us through the lives of God's people

When Paul tells us that *all Scripture is useful for teaching* this clearly shows that God speaks to us not only by the passages that give us direct instructions as to what to do, but also by narrative passages that give us examples from the lives of God's people in the past. For example, in 1 Corinthians 10 we read:

---

[25] Always bearing in mind, of course, the lessons we learned in Chapter 4 about the importance of examining the context of what we're reading.

Now these things occurred as examples to keep us from setting our hearts on evil things as they did (6).

These things happened to them as examples and were written down as warnings for us, on whom the fulfillment of the ages has come. So, if you think you are standing firm, be careful that you don't fall (11-12).

In this passage Paul is warning the Corinthians against the sins of idol worship, sexual immorality and grumbling (vv. 7-10) and he does so by reminding them of what happened to God's people in the Old Testament when they were guilty of these things. He uses a Bible story from the Old Testament to warn New Testament Christians of the need to live holy lives.

In a similar way, we can learn not only from the lives of God's people in the Old Testament, but we can read the New Testament accounts of the lives of Jesus' disciples and learn from their mistakes. As we read about Thomas and his doubts, we see that he did not really need to doubt, and God speaks to us through the story and encourages our faith. And we can all probably identify with Peter and see in his shortcomings a picture of our own. But we also learn how Jesus forgave him and showed him that he still had a purpose for his life.

So Bible stories are not just there to warn us. They are more often there in order to inspire us, to encourage and comfort us. In Romans 15:4 Paul tells us that everything that was written in the past was written to teach us, so that through endurance and the encouragement of the Scriptures we might have hope.

Who, for example, has not been inspired and encouraged by the faith and heroism recorded in the story of David and Goliath? Of course, we know from the New Testament that today our battle is not against flesh and blood but against the spiritual forces of evil in the heavenly realms (Ephesians 6:12), but although the enemy may be different the principles of victory remain the same. God speaks to us in both Old and New Testaments through the accounts of his dealings with his people[26]

So God speaks to us through the lives of God's people in the past and it's even possible that we learn more from them than we do from the passages that contain direct instructions to us. At the very least they shed light on the meaning of these passages. This is particularly true of the story of the early church as it's recorded in the book of Acts. If all Scripture is useful for teaching - and Acts is certainly Scripture - then we can surely learn that the kind of things God did back then are just what we should be expecting today.

I shall always be grateful to Laurie Dixon, the man who first told me about the baptism in the Holy Spirit, for challenging me to read the book of Acts and ask myself how the life and practices of the church I was attending measured up to the experience of the early disciples. That challenge was to radically alter the entire direction of the ministry to which God had called me.

Although I didn't realise it at the time, Laurie's challenge involved a very important issue of hermeneutics – the principles by which we interpret Scripture. The New Testament epistles are largely comprised of direct instruction, but I believe that some of the teaching found in them can only be understood correctly by reading the narrative passages in the Gospels and Acts.

---

[26] I give numerous examples of this in a series of podcasts entitled *Lessons from their Lives.* For details visit www.davidpetts.org

For example, in Ephesians 5:18 we're encouraged to be filled with the Spirit. But what exactly does it mean to be filled with the Spirit? The immediate context in Ephesians does not make this completely clear. That's almost certainly because Paul knew that his readers would have understood exactly what he meant by it.

But that doesn't help us very much. However, as we read the book of Acts we see several examples of people being filled with the Spirit. These examples paint a clear picture for us of what Paul means when he tells us to be filled with the Spirit. We learn that Paul is referring to a supernatural experience that is received suddenly rather than gradually and is accompanied by miraculous gifts that greatly empower our witness for Christ [27].

A similar example might be what it means to be baptised. Jesus commanded his disciples to *make disciples of all nations, baptising them in the name of the Father and of the Son and of the Holy Spirit* (Matthew 28:19-21). But what does it mean to be baptised? As we read the accounts of people being baptised in the Gospels and Acts we see that there is no suggestion that baptism was by sprinkling.

Apart from the fact that the Greek verb *baptizo* means *immerse* and not *sprinkle*, the descriptions of people being baptised strongly indicate that baptism was always by immersion. To give just one example, in the story of Philip baptising the Ethiopian eunuch (Acts 8:36-39) we're told that both Philip and the eunuch *went down into*

---

[27] For more on this, see *A New Dimension - how to be filled with the Holy Spirit*. For details visit www.davidpetts.org

the water and that after the baptism they both *came up out of the water*. This surely implies immersion rather than sprinkling[28].

However, my purpose in saying this is not to argue the merits of baptism by immersion, but rather to illustrate how narrative passages in the Bible can shed light on what is meant by the terminology used elsewhere. The examples I have used show how Acts can provide a visual aid for us which helps us understand the terminology used in the epistles.

But that is not all. A distinction is sometimes made between the passages of scripture that are *descriptive* and those that are *prescriptive*. The narrative passages in the Gospel and Acts, for example, are seen as descriptive. They describe what happened. But the teaching in the epistles is referred to as prescriptive. It prescribes what we should believe and how we should behave.

On this basis, some have argued that descriptive passages are not really suitable as a source of doctrine. Yet the major doctrine of the Christian faith, the resurrection of Christ from the dead, is based largely on the description we have in the four Gospels!

Furthermore, it seems to me that descriptive passages can at times have prescriptive value. Of course, when I describe an incident I am not necessarily prescribing a course of action. But when I am in a teaching situation and I describe not just one event, but several, and all those events have certain features in common, my students may legitimately assume that my intention is not just descriptive but that it is also prescriptive.

---

[28] For more detailed discussion of this, see *You'd Better Believe It,* Chapter 13. Details from www.davidpetts.org

For example, if I relate how I handled certain cases in the course of my pastoral ministry, and in connection with each case I mention that I prayed for guidance in that situation, my students would be right to assume that my intention is to teach them that they too should pray in similar situations. I am in effect teaching by example. This is a powerful didactic method which may well be far more effective than straight instruction. Understood this way the narrative passages in the Gospels and Acts really can teach us a great deal[29].

So let's remember that God speaks to us throughout Scripture and as we read the historical accounts of God's dealings with his people, and especially the lives of the early disciples after Pentecost, God may well challenge us, or encourage and inspire us. The things that happened to them are written as examples for us.

---

[29] I have argued this at some length in my article *The Baptism in the Holy Spirit,* in *Pentecostal Perspectives*, Warrington, K. (ed.), Carlisle, Paternoster, 1998.

CHAPTER SIX

Directions

So far we have identified three ways in which God speaks to us through the Bible. He encourages us by the promises he has made. He shows us what to believe and how to behave. And through the lives of God's people in the Bible he teaches us what to expect. We now turn our attention to how God sometimes directs us by bringing key verses to our attention.

Now we need to tread very carefully here. We have already seen the importance of understanding Bible verses in the context in which they are written. Taking a verse out of its context can lead to wrong conclusions about what God is saying and even to seriously wrong actions if the following anecdotal story is to be believed.

A young Christian, who was feeling the need of encouragement, opened the Bible at random looking for a word from the Lord. It fell open at Matthew 27:5 where he read that Judas *went and hanged himself.* As he did not find this very encouraging, he thought he would try again. This time the Bible fell open at Luke 10:37 where to his dismay he read, *Go and do likewise!* So he tried again and read in John 13:27, *What you are about to do, do quickly.*

Now I'm pretty sure this story is apocryphal. If it isn't, it's to be hoped that the young man did not act upon what he read. However, I suspect that the story was made up to illustrate the danger of taking verses out of their context, and the point is well made. Nevertheless, I'm sure that many Christians have had similar experiences to me, where God has spoken very clearly through Bible verses taken completely out of context. I'm now going to give you a few examples from my own experience and although, admittedly, I'm not sure we can find any parallel examples in Scripture, I hope to show you that there are times when God can and does speak to us in this way and I'll suggest some guidelines on how to be sure we're hearing the Lord correctly.

During my first year as a student at Oxford I was asked by my tutor to write an essay on the ontological argument for the existence of God. This was one of the arguments used, for example, by the philosopher René Descartes in an attempt to prove God's existence. During the course of my essay I said something to the effect that although philosophy cannot prove the existence of God it cannot disprove it either.

It was at this point, as I was reading my essay to my tutor, that he interrupted me by saying:

> Oh, I don't know. I think if you mean by 'prove' what we normally mean by 'prove', and if you mean by 'God' what we normally mean by 'God', then we can probably disprove God's existence. But perhaps we can talk about it another time

This was the first time in my life that I had been confronted with such an outright denial of God's existence, and my tutor's statement shocked me deeply. It challenged everything I had based my life upon. I felt numb. As soon as he had left the room I instinctively wanted to call out to God for help. But what if my tutor was right and there was no God to call out to? But I called out anyway:

> God, if there is a God, HELP!

And He did! I walked into my bedroom and picked up my Bible and opened it. It fell open at Psalm 119, verse 99. My teacher had told me that he could prove that there is no God. Who was I to challenge the statement of an Oxford tutor? But in that verse the Psalmist said:

> *I have more insight than all my teachers, for I meditate on your statutes.*

I came later to realise that by reading the Bible the most simple believer can gain more understanding of the things that really matter than all the intellectual rationalising of the philosopher. That verse brought immediate reassurance to my heart. It was not just the content of the verse that reassured me – though it certainly did – but the fact that, of all the verses in the Bible I should turn at random to that very one. This was surely no coincidence.

Just over ten years later, in January 1972, while I was pastoring a church in Basingstoke, I was also a visiting lecturer at Kenley Bible College in Surrey. The College later moved to Nottinghamshire and became known as Mattersey Hall Bible College where I eventually became the Principal.

During one of my fortnightly visits to Kenley I learned that one of the full-time lecturers was leaving at the end of the academic year. I naturally wondered who might be chosen to replace him. I was thinking about this as I was driving home that evening and I wondered for a moment if they might ask me. But I quickly dismissed the thought as I believed that God wanted me to stay in Basingstoke and build a big church. However, I said to God as I was driving along:

> *Of course, if ever You want me to move to the College and work there, I will. But please make it very clear that that is what You want me to do.*

That night I woke up at about 2 o'clock in the morning with a burning conviction that I was going to the Bible College. I tried to shake it off, but the conviction would not leave me. I tried telling myself that there was a simple psychological explanation. It was because of what I had been thinking about before I went to bed. But I couldn't get back to sleep and, remembering what I had said to God in the car coming home, I decided to go downstairs and pray.

I poured myself a glass of milk from the fridge and then said to God:

> Lord, You know I need my sleep, so if You're trying to tell me something, please talk to me quickly so that I can go back to bed

Looking back on it, I'm surprised that I dared to talk to the Almighty like that, but that is what I said. Then, thinking that it might help if I read something from the Bible I opened it at random. It fell open at 2 Chronicles 34:22 which, in the Authorised Version of the Bible I was using at the time, referred to Huldah the prophetess who DWELT IN THE COLLEGE in Jerusalem.

I did not even know that the word *college* was in the Bible. But as I was seriously asking God if He wanted me to live and work at the Bible College, the first verse I turned to as I opened my Bible contained the words *dwelt at the college.* This surely could be no coincidence? Yet that is what at first I thought it must be. I couldn't really believe that they would want me full time at the College. I had all kind of objections to the whole idea, not least of which was that I thought they would say I was too young.

But as I made my objections, one by one God answered them by directing me to verses that showed me I had no good reason for making such excuses. By the time God had finished with me that night I knew without a shadow of a doubt that I would one day live and work at the College. But I did not know then that I would be its Principal for 27 years (1977-2004).

When the time came for me to retire from Mattersey and move on to an even wider international ministry, I was naturally concerned that the right person be appointed as my successor. During my principalship, with God's help and the able assistance of a gifted and dedicated team, the number of students had more than trebled, we had erected a wonderful new Hall of Residence and a beautiful new chapel and classrooms, we were offering a range of university validated courses, and, most important of all, we had prepared hundreds of students to spread the message of the gospel throughout the world. It was, therefore, vitally important that the right person be appointed to build on the foundation we had laid.

But I had no idea who that person should be. I could think of a few names of people who might well be suitable, but who was the person chosen by God? I did not know. Surely this was time for a clear word from the Lord. However, the decision was not mine to make. I was one of a committee who would interview candidates and then recommend to the National Leadership Team (NLT) who should be nominated for appointment.

Nevertheless, I was conscious that my opinion would be well respected, and I felt a burden of responsibility to come to a decision as to whom I would recommend if I were asked. But on the day before the NLT were due to meet I still had no clear word from the Lord. But then, why should I expect one as the decision was not mine to make?

Then something happened very similar to what took place in 1972 when the Lord first showed me that I was going to work at the Bible

College. That night I woke up at about 2 a.m. and could not get back to sleep. The issue of who should be my successor was playing on my mind. So I said something like this:

> Lord, I don't know who it should be. I don't even know if I need to know. It's not my responsibility to make the decision. Please help.

Then I picked up a Bible. It fell open at the first chapter of the Song of Songs. In the version I was reading, verse 8 says:

> My dearest, if you don't know, just follow the path of the sheep.

I felt the Lord was saying that, since I *didn't know* who my successor should be, I should simply *follow* the decision that would be made by God's people (*the sheep*) who were to be meeting the next day. The Lord then gave me Psalm 125:3 which assured me that he wouldn't let the wrong person lead his people and Matthew 6:34 telling me not to worry about tomorrow.

Now I need to make it very clear that I do not recommend opening a Bible at random as a regular means of getting guidance from God. The Bible is God's word and He does speak to us through it, but to understand what He is saying we should read it in context. I have spent the last 50 years of my life trying to teach Christians to do just that!

However, there are rare occasions when a verse of the Bible seems to leap out of the page at you and God speaks to you through it even though the original intention of the verse may have been entirely different.

But when this happens how can we be sure that we are hearing what God is saying correctly? We're not now talking about the guidelines we gave earlier on how to understand the Bible correctly. Those guidelines relate mainly to what we should believe and teach. But when we feel that God is speaking to us directly and guiding us personally through the words of a Bible text, other guidelines are appropriate.

The basic principle is that **we should not rely on the words we have read to guide us without seeking confirmation**. This can come in various ways. Let's use the example of the call to the Bible College that I received in 1972. The first thing to notice is that I already had an *inner conviction* that I was going to live at the college.

Secondly, the verse containing the words *dwelt at the college* was *not the only verse* God gave me that night. I was given several other verses that supported it. What's more, it was *not out of line with the overall teaching of Scripture*. The promptings of the Spirit will always be in harmony with the principles taught in the Bible.

Thirdly, my call to the college was *tested by other people*, first by confidential discussion with senior church leaders and ultimately by the vote of confidence given by a conference of ministers.

Fourthly, the task to which God was calling me was totally suited to the *natural and spiritual gifts* he had given me.

And fifthly, the calling was *tested by time*. It was not until five years later in 1977 that I became acting principal and not until 1978 that the appointment was finally confirmed.

These five safeguards will ensure that we are hearing God correctly when we feel that God has spoken to us through a random verse of scripture. You may not receive confirmation in all these ways, but at least you should receive it by some of them. I will be developing these principles in Chapter 16 when we talk about other ways God guides us.

PART THREE

GOD SPEAKS THROUGH OTHER PEOPLE

CHAPTER SEVEN

Parents

So far, all that we have said has centred very much around the Bible. We have said that God speaks to us through the person of Jesus, but what we know about Jesus we derive from the Bible. We have also considered various ways in which God speaks to us directly through the Bible, but now we turn our attention to other ways in which God speaks to us.

We'll start by looking at how he speaks to us through other people. But even here our knowledge of what the Bible teaches will be vital. Well-meaning people can get things wrong and anything they say must be filtered through our understanding of what the Bible has to say.

Of course, God can speak through anyone he wants to – he once even spoke through a donkey (Numbers 22)! But in the next few chapters we'll be concentrating on four major categories of people through whom the Lord may speak to us – parents, other Christians, preachers, pastors, and prophets. As usual I'll be illustrating what the Bible has to say with examples from my own personal experience.

The Bible is very clear in its teaching that children should learn from their parents about the things of God. We are told to honour our parents, to obey our parents, and to heed their instruction. It follows, therefore, that one way that God has chosen to speak to us is through the instruction and advice of our parents. It is our parents' responsibility to explain to us the truth about God, to show us by their teaching and example the difference between right and wrong, and to advise us as to the best course of action when we are unsure of what we should do.

I am personally very grateful to God that my parents fulfilled that role in a wonderful way, but I am very conscious that not all my readers will have had Christian parents and that some may have had a very different experience from mine. My wife, Eileen, is one example of this.

Her parents, despite many good qualities, were by no means ideal, but they did send her to Sunday school and at the age of seven Eileen was led to the Lord by her Sunday school teacher. Since that day she has always sought to be the kind of person God would want her to be, and was determined that, when she became a mother, she would be a better parent to our children than her parents had been to her.

The fact that our three children, who are now in their fifties, have all grown up to love and serve the Lord is in my view largely due Eileen's godly influence. So, if you did not enjoy the benefit of ideal parents, please remember that the Lord can help you to be a better parent to your children than they were to you.

However, as I have said, my experience was very different from Eileen's. I remember how, at the age of eight, I was sitting on my father's knee when I asked him,

Daddy, how good do you have to be to go to Heaven?

I think the question was on my mind because of something that was called **David's good boy chart**. This was a chart my father had made, rather like a calendar, with a space for each day for him to stick on it a coloured sun or moon or star, depending on how my behaviour had been that day. I think he had made it because my mother had been having some problems with me during the day while he was at work. When he got home, my mother would tell him how I had behaved that day and an appropriate sticker would be applied to the chart. If I'd been good, it would be a sun, not so good, a moon, and so on. I think I must have been wondering how many suns I would need if I wanted to go to Heaven!

My father explained that it wasn't a question of how good we are, because none of us is good enough to go to Heaven. That's why Jesus came to die on the cross to take the punishment for our sins so that all who believe in him would have everlasting life. Then he asked,

Do you believe that, David?

I replied, *Yes, of course I do.*

And why do you believe it? asked my father.

Because you have told me, I said.

That's a good reason, he said, *but one day you will come to believe it for yourself.*

That's the first time I can remember that I was consciously aware of the truth of the gospel. I suppose that, like many who have been brought up in a Christian home, I can't put a date on when I first believed. It feels as though I have always believed. I cannot remember a time when I did not believe. I used to be concerned about this, especially when so many Christians can remember a specific date.

But then I heard an illustration that was very helpful and which at the time of writing this chapter was particularly relevant because Eileen and I were celebrating our 60th wedding anniversary that very week.

Now I have never forgotten our wedding anniversary, but even if one year I had, I would never have forgotten that I am married and who I am married to!

The point of the illustration is this. The date that my married relationship with Eileen started is relatively unimportant compared with our relationship *now*. The same applies to our relationship with Jesus. What matters is not when our relationship started, but am I in relationship with him *now*? Am I trusting him *now* for the forgiveness of my sins and my home in heaven? And if I am, then the exact date it all started is relatively unimportant.

So I cannot remember an exact date when I first believed. But I can remember the day when I decided to give my life to Christ. And again, it was through my father that I came to that decision. Every Sunday afternoon my father used to teach the teenage Bible class in our Baptist church. I remember sitting listening to him week after week talking from John 3:16. The challenge was not so much, *Did I believe?* but rather, *What would I do about it?*

I decided that, if God loved me so much that he sent his Son to die on the cross to save me from my sins, the least I could do was to give my life to him. So the next time our pastor made an appeal for those who would surrender to Christ and obey him by being baptised in water, I walked forward in response and was baptised on July 19th 1953.

So it was through my father's teaching and my mother's example and encouragement that I became a Christian. As we have said, one of the ways God speaks to us is through our parents and the most solemn responsibility of every Christian parent is to show their children the way of salvation.

But there are other ways too that God uses our parents to speak to us. The book of Proverbs emphasises again and again the wisdom of paying attention to the advice of our parents and in both Old and New Testaments we are told to honour our father and mother. And surely if we honour and respect them we will be grateful for the advice they give us.

Of course, when we are young children and not yet mature enough to make wise decisions for ourselves, it's appropriate that our parents should *tell* us what to do. We should *obey* them. But when we are mature adults it's not so much a question of obedience as of honouring them and listening to their advice.

And in between our childhood and our adulthood we have the period of adolescence. This is a time of transitioning from obedience to honouring and I am grateful for my parents' wisdom in encouraging me as a teenager to make my own decisions while at the same time offering their advice as to what might well be the right course of action to take.

One example of this was when, at the age of 12, I had to decide whether to opt for studying Greek or German at school. My father pointed out that if I opted for Greek it might help me if, in the future, I needed to study the New Testament in greater depth. Within three years I was translating parts of the Greek New Testament and eventually taught Greek for many years in our Bible College. Neither my father nor I could possibly have known this, but I believe that through my father the Lord was directing my steps according to his plan for my life.

A few years later, at the age of 17, I was offered a scholarship to read P.P.E. (Philosophy, Politics and Economics) at Brasenose College,

Oxford. A year before this I had already felt a call to serve the Lord as a minister and, when I received the news about the scholarship, I was initially unsure as to whether I should accept it. Perhaps I should be applying to Bible College instead?

I asked my father what he thought, and he suggested that I should take into consideration that God might well have a purpose in my going to Oxford, especially bearing in mind that places at Oxford were pretty hard to come by! As I look back, I'm glad I took my father's advice. I was baptised in the Holy Spirit just four weeks before starting my course at Oxford and was used by the Lord in spreading the Pentecostal testimony to other students and conducting Bible studies and prayer meetings seeking spiritual gifts.

The type of degree I was reading was relatively unimportant. I knew I was at the right place in the right time. And my Oxford degree has opened doors for me that might not have been open had I studied elsewhere, including invitations to speak in universities and colleges not only in Britain, but further afield in Europe, Africa and the United States.

So in this chapter I have tried to show firstly from Scripture and then from my personal experience that one way that God speaks to us is through our parents. Much of what I have said has related to my father who, in my early years, clearly had a very great influence on my life for which I will always been grateful to God.

But ultimately we must decide for ourselves what the Lord is saying to us, whoever it might be that he has chosen to speak through. And that applies not only to parents but also to the preachers and pastors and prophets, and indeed the many other people through whom he may choose to speak to us.

CHAPTER EIGHT

Other Christians

I suppose that if we were to ask most Christians who it is they expect God to use in speaking to them, their answer would almost certainly include preachers or pastors or prophets. And we will be dealing with these later. But it's very important that we should realise that God often speaks through Christians who do not come into any of these categories.

Of course, there are those who are especially gifted by God to speak for him. Ephesians 4:11, for example, mentions apostles, prophets, evangelists, pastors and teachers. But the New Testament also makes it clear that God expects *all* his people to speak for him. As I have pointed out elsewhere, there is a sense in which all God's people are prophets[30]. The Holy Spirit can use anyone he chooses.

For example, the great church at Antioch was first started by ordinary Christians spreading the word. In Acts 8:1-4 we read that, as a result of the persecution that followed the death of Stephen, the Christians were scattered throughout Judea and Samaria. But they spread the word wherever they went (v.4). Acts 11:19-21 tells us:

> *Now those who had been scattered by the persecution in connection with Stephen traveled as far as Phoenicia, Cyprus and Antioch, telling the message only to Jews.*

---

[30] See *Body Builders – Gifts to make God's people grow,* Chapter 3.
I will be referring to this again on page 120.

Some of them, however, men from Cyprus and Cyrene, went to Antioch and began to speak to Greeks also, telling them the good news about the Lord Jesus.

The Lord's hand was with them, and a great number of people believed and turned to the Lord.

This church was founded, not by the apostles, who had all remained in Jerusalem (Acts 8:2), but by ordinary Christians spreading the good news of the gospel. God can speak *through* any one of us, and he can speak *to* any one of us by whomever he chooses, as the following examples from my own experience demonstrate.

I have already mentioned Laurie Dixon whose testimony changed the course of my life. The year before I met Laurie, I was on holiday in the Lake District at a Baptist Summer School where I made friends with a young man named Michael Stewart. Michael told me that the following year he was planning with a couple of Christian friends to take a car and visit several countries in Europe. He asked if I would be interested in joining them. Travelling abroad was far less common in those days than it is today, and I jumped at the opportunity.

So, in 1958 I found myself in Switzerland with Michael and three new friends climbing a mountain. The long climb in the heat of the August sunshine had been tiring. We were unaccustomed to this kind of exercise and the cool water of the mountain stream was inviting to our aching feet. Graham, Michael, and Daphne sat down to rest, putting their feet in the water.

But it was my first visit to Switzerland, and somehow I felt that we were wasting an opportunity when there was so much to see. Leaving the others to paddle their feet, Laurie and I climbed higher following the path of the stream, but half an hour later we had had enough too. As we looked down at the others a few hundred feet below us, we realised that we had come up the hard way. To our right there was an easier way down.

Gratefully we turned to take it, when suddenly, as if from nowhere, a large rock came hurtling down the mountainside toward the stream and I was directly in its path! As a fairly athletic nineteen-year-old, I should have been able to jump clear with relative ease, but I was gripped with terror, unable to move.

As a Christian I might have thought of praying, but my mind refused to function. In a second it would hit me. The end had surely come. But when the rock was only about a yard away, it struck a small protusion in the ground, changed direction, and crashed into the stream below, missing me by inches! The danger was over as quickly as it had come.

I heaved a sigh of inexpressible relief.

> *Wow that was lucky!* I exclaimed.

> *Lucky, David?*

said Laurie who'd been watching from a few yards away.

> *That wasn't luck. I believe God has a purpose for your life and that rock **couldn't** have hit you.*

It was that simple statement of faith that started a process of enquiry which was to lead to an experience which revolutionised my life. This man was moving in a dimension of Christianity that I knew little or nothing about. So I questioned Laurie to see if I could discover the basic difference.

Although from different denominational backgrounds, I discovered that we had much in common. Doctrinally, our beliefs were almost identical. We believed the same Bible, preached the same gospel, and worshipped the same Saviour. We both knew what it meant to be a born-again Christian. We had both been baptised as believers by immersion in water. Basically, we had very much in common. And yet this man had something which I didn't have, something indefinable, but very real. I asked him what it was.

He started to talk about an experience he had received after his conversion - *being baptised with the Holy Spirit* he called it - when the Holy Spirit had come and filled him to overflowing. He said he had *spoken in tongues* and told me I could read about it in the book of Acts.

It was at this point, however, that my interest began to wane. I certainly wanted to experience more of God in my life, but as for speaking in tongues, I frankly couldn't see the point of it. If being *baptised with the Holy Spirit* meant that I had to speak in tongues, I decided that I had better forget about it.

And for a while I did! On returning to England, I dismissed the subject from my mind and might have ignored it forever, had it not been for the remarkable series of events which took place the following summer when both Eileen and I were baptised in the Spirit. But that's a story that can wait until another chapter!

So God used Laurie Dixon to speak to me. This was not only by his words but also by his actions. No doubt we're all familiar with the expression, *Actions speak louder than words*. Less well known is the Latin motto, *Facta non verba*, which means, *Deeds not words*. We've already seen how God speaks to us through Jesus both by what he said and what he did. His actions as much as his words show us what God is like and how he wants us to behave. And this is how he often speaks to us today

A good example of God speaking to me through the actions of another Christian is our friend Jill Cooper who used to help Eileen serve coffee on Sunday mornings at our local church. What she did was incredibly simple, but before I tell you what it was, I need to give you the background story.

In February 2010 Eileen and I went to India for a month at the invitation of the Finnish Pentecostal Churches who asked me to go and teach about the Holy Spirit where they had missionaries working in Mumbai and Machilipatnam. Now while I was the Principal at Mattersey Hall Bible College we had the privilege of training many overseas students several of whom were from India, and when our former students heard about our trip, they were quick to ask us if we would visit them too so that I could preach in the numerous churches they had planted since returning from Mattersey.

We, of course, were delighted to agree, but I knew that the schedule they organized for me would be quite intense and, as I have always believed in observing a Sabbath principle, I asked that one day in seven should be a rest day. However, in practice this didn't happen, as the day they scheduled as a rest day was the day we had to travel from one place to the next! As a result, and because that year the temperature in India was higher than usual, I was suffering from dehydration and to the disappointment of all concerned, a few of the meetings scheduled had to be cancelled.

Apart from this, we had had a great time in India and after a few weeks back in England I thought I had fully recovered. But towards the end of April, on a preaching trip to Essex, I started to experience similar symptoms to those I'd had in India. I couldn't understand this as the temperature in England was about half what it had been in India. Without going into unnecessary detail, the next two years proved to be extremely difficult. I continued to experience similar problems every time I preached. I began to wonder if the time had come for me to give up.

Then, at just the right time, Eileen and I were in Exeter at a meeting for Assemblies of God ministers and their wives. The guest preacher was John Glass, the General Superintendent of the Elim Churches. He was preaching on Jeremiah 1 when he came to verses 11-12:

> The word of the LORD came to me: "What do you see, Jeremiah?" "I see the branch of an **almond** tree," I replied. The LORD said to me, "You have seen correctly, for I am **watching** to see that my word is fulfilled."

He explained the play on words that we find in these verses – the Hebrew word for *almond* is very similar to the word for *watch*. The almond tree is among the first to blossom in spring. It's something you watch for as a sign that spring has come. Winter will surely be followed by spring because God watches over his word to see that it is fulfilled.

Now in England most of us don't see an almond tree too often, so John likened it to crocuses. In his garden they're the first flowers to bloom in spring. They're the sign or guarantee that winter won't be forever. Then John broke away from his notes and said something like this:

> There are some of you here who are feeling that your ministry has come to an end. You have been experiencing a bleak

winter, but the Lord wants you to know that it will not be forever. You will experience a new springtime.

Eileen and I looked at each other. Was this for us? Surely it must be. But there were a lot of other people in that meeting. Could it be that John's prophetic word was for them and not for us? We drove home after the meeting hoping, rather than believing, that this really was a word from the Lord for us.

And then, that evening, Jill Cooper arrived on our doorstep and said,

I've brought you a little present. To be honest, I had bought it for someone else, but then I felt the Lord tell me to give it to you instead.

What was the present? A bowl of *crocuses*!

And without a doubt, I have experienced a new springtime in my ministry. So the Lord does speak to us through other Christians, both by their words and by their actions. And, as the story I have just told you clearly illustrates, he most certainly speaks to us through preachers.

CHAPTER NINE

Preachers and Pastors

So far we have considered how God speaks to us through our parents and through other Christians. We now turn our attention to how God speaks to us through the preaching of his word by those he has called and gifted to do so. We have already seen that God expects all Christians to spread the good news of the gospel to those with whom they come in contact. The gift of the Holy Spirit is available to all Christians and his empowering enables us all to be witnesses for Christ.

In Ephesians 4:11-12, however, we read how Christ has given to the church apostles, prophets, evangelists, pastors and teachers, to equip God's people for works of service so that the body of Christ may be built up. I have written at length on each of these roles in my book, *Body Builders*, so won't be going into great detail here. It will be enough for us to remind ourselves that one of the chief ways that God has chosen to speak to us is through his servants.

Of course, God speaks to us individually as we read our Bibles, but that by no means does away with the need for the teaching of God's word through those to whom he has entrusted our spiritual welfare. In Acts 20 the apostle Paul is on his way to Jerusalem and at Miletus he calls for the elders of the church to come and see him (v17). He knows that none of them will ever see him again (v25) and he wants to encourage them and pray with them one last time. He tells them to:

Keep watch over yourselves and all the flock of which the Holy Spirit has made you overseers. Be shepherds of the church of God, which he bought with his own blood (v28).

Notice that in verse 17 these people are referred to as elders. In this verse they're called overseers and shepherds. It's clear from this and from passages like 1 Peter 5:1-5 and Titus 1:5-7 that:

- In the New Testament elders, overseers, and shepherds (pastors) are interchangeable terms referring to the same role.

- Their responsibility is to protect and care for the flock (God's people) from 'wolves' (false teachers) who distort the truth (Acts 20:29, 1 Peter 5:2).

- They must encourage others by sound teaching and refute those who oppose it (Titus 1:9).

- They are ultimately accountable to Christ, who is the Chief Shepherd of the flock (1 Peter 5:5).

Since God has given such a serious responsibility to those who are the shepherds of his sheep, it follows that his people are to pay attention to the teaching and advice given by church leaders. I can't say in all honestly that I have always done so – in fact I remember that as a teenager I sometimes argued publicly with our Baptist pastor (for which I wrote and apologized a few years later after I was baptized with the Holy Spirit). But I'm so glad that down through the years again and again God has spoken to me and guided me through the teaching and advice of pastors and other preachers.

Perhaps the best example of this is how the Lord called me to full-time ministry. Mamhead Park is a country mansion built regardless of cost in the nineteenth century. Set in hundreds of acres of beautiful countryside, with views going down to the sea at Lyme Bay on the south coast of England, in the 1950s it was used by the Baptists as a centre for retreats and conferences. It was also used in the school holidays for Summer Schools for young people. It was at one of these that God spoke to me and showed me that I was to be a minister[31].

It was at the end of one of the evening sessions. The preacher had just finished his message and the Reverend Cyril Rushbridge, who had been leading the meeting, was expected to close in prayer. But before he did so, he said,

> *Before we close in prayer I just feel the Lord wants me to tell you how he called me to the ministry.*

He then took just a few minutes sharing with us how this had happened. It was nothing like Paul's experience on the Damascus Road. I don't remember the details, but by the time he had finished I felt sure that God was calling me to the ministry too. This was confirmed by Kate, one of the young people from our youth group, who said to me as soon as the meeting ended,

> *David, do you know now what the Lord wants you to do with your life?*

The answer was yes, I was absolutely sure.

---

[31] There is a sense, of course, in which all God's people are ministers, but I am using the word here, in the sense in which I understood it back then, and as many churches still understand it today, to mean the full-time pastor of a local church.

I wrote home to my parents telling them what had happened. When I got home, they told me how pleased they were and how, when the doctor had told them that they were unlikely to have any children, they had prayed that the Lord would give them a son who would have an international ministry.

I was 16 at the time and in the middle of preparing for A levels at school. I spoke to our pastor, the Reverend Leslie Moxham, and asked his advice as to my next steps now that the Lord had called me to the ministry. He suggested that I should start to attend the midweek Prayer and Bible Study meeting and this I was happy to do. But there was just one problem – time!

Students at Brentwood School, where I attended, had lessons for six days every week and were expected to do two to three hours 'prep' every evening. Sunday was the only day we were not at school and on Sundays I was already attending Boys' Brigade Bible Class at 10am, the morning church service at 11am, teenage Bible Class at 3pm, youth discussion group at 4.30pm, the evening service at 6.30pm and an after church 'sing-song' from 8-9pm! I also attended Boys' Brigade, Young People's Fellowship, and the church Youth Club three evenings every week. Could I still fit in an extra meeting without it affecting my studies at school?

My history teacher clearly thought not! About two months before I was due to take my A level exams, he said to me in front of the whole class,

> *Quite honestly, Petts, unless you work harder, you're going to fail your A levels.*

To which I replied,

Well, you see Sir, I believe that God has called me to the ministry and that it's important that I attend the meetings at our church,

and I explained to him how busy I was. Then I added,

Actually, Sir, I believe that if I put God first, and if he wants me to pass my A levels, he will not let me down.

To which he replied,

Petts, I respect your convictions, but I can't say that I agree with you.

As a result of that conversation, I did try to work harder, but I also continued to attend all the meetings at church, including the midweek Bible Study recommended by my pastor. When the A level results were published, to the surprise of my teacher I had received a comfortable pass in all subjects, including History.

And to my surprise, I was shortly afterwards awarded a prestigious Heseltine Exhibition to study at Brasenose College, Oxford. I give God all the glory for this. I had followed my Pastor's advice and had tried to put God first. I had honoured the Lord in front of my teacher and fellow-students, and the Lord did not fail me.

A few years later, after graduating from Oxford, I was pastoring a small church in Colchester. The church funds were insufficient to pay me full time, so I was teaching Religious Education in a local secondary school to provide for the needs of our young family. This was clearly part of the Lord's plan as during the years I was teaching there dozens of teenagers came to our church and made decisions for Christ. But I knew that the Lord had called me to full time ministry and that eventually the time would come for me to give up my teaching job. The question was, when?

The answer came during the Assemblies of God Annual Conference held in Clacton in May 1966. I was not able to attend during the day as it coincided with the school summer term, but I was able to go in the evenings as Clacton is not very far from Colchester. The preacher on the first night was Pastor Eddie Durham. He began by talking about how, in time past, if a man wanted to challenge another to a duel, he would throw down a gauntlet in front of him. The challenge was accepted by the other man picking up the gauntlet. Pastor Durham then produced a motorcycle gauntlet and threw in on the floor before the congregation, saying,

> *I challenge young men in this meeting to give themselves full time to the ministry!*

I remember thinking,

> *That's all very well. I'd love to be full time in the ministry, but it simply isn't possible financially.*

My teaching job was our only means of income. But then I added,

> *But, Lord, if that's what you want me to do, I'll do it, but you'll have to make it very clear by the end of the week.*

The reason I said this was that I was contractually obliged to submit my resignation to the school where I was teaching by the end of May if I was not going to return for the beginning of the new term in September. God had just a week to let me know what he wanted me to do.

And he did! Night after night I went back to those meetings, having told no one but Eileen what I had prayed. And each night, in one way or another, God spoke to me confirming that I was to give up my teaching job.

A particular highlight was the preaching of Thomas F. Zimmerman, the General Superintendent of Assemblies of God in the USA, who was one of the guest preachers at the conference. What made it particularly significant was the fact that it was the night of my ordination where hands were laid on me in recognition of the ministry God had given me[32]. Zimmerman's message was based on 1 Kings 17-18 and the story of Elijah. I was reminded that if we follow God's PLAN, we will know his PROVISION and his POWER.

By the end of the week Eileen and I were fully convinced that God's plan was that I should give up my teaching job and trust him to provide for our needs. And so, first thing on Monday morning, I went to the head teacher, who, incidentally, was an atheist, and handed in my resignation. When asked for a reason, I could only reply,

> Well Sir, this may sound a little strange, but God has told me to.

---

[32] I was pleased to discover that the two senior ministers who laid hands on me and prayed for me were John Nelson Parr and Howard Carter, both of whom were key pioneers in the history of the Pentecostal Movement.

CHAPTER TEN

Prophets and Prophecy

So God speaks to us through pastors and preachers, but he also speaks to us through prophets and the gift of prophecy. We'll begin by explaining what prophecy is. In the English language the word *prophet* is often used to refer to someone who foretells the future. But its basic meaning is *someone who speaks on behalf of someone else.* A good illustration of this can be found in Exodus 7:1-2. Here the Lord says to Moses:

> *See, I have made you like God to Pharaoh, and your brother Aaron will be your prophet. You are to say everything I command you, and your brother Aaron is to tell Pharaoh to let the Israelites go...*

Aaron is called Moses' prophet because he is going to speak on his behalf. So prophets are people who speak on behalf of God. They hear from God and then pass on to others what he has said. Moving now to the New Testament, we find that there are three different levels at which prophecy may operate:

- There is a sense in which all God's people are prophets (Acts 2:16-18)

- Prophecy as a spiritual gift is given to some Christians, but not all (1 Corinthians 12:8-11).

- Prophets are given to the church to equip God's people for works of service (Ephesians 4:11-12).

119

All God's people are prophets

As we've already seen, a prophet is a person who speaks on behalf of God. Understood this way it is easy to see how, in a sense, all God's people are prophets. We are all called to speak on his behalf. As the children of God, it is our privilege to be led by the Spirit of God (Romans 8:14) and the purpose of the Spirit's coming at Pentecost was that we might receive power to be witnesses (Acts 1:8). The Spirit was poured out so that all God's people could prophesy – sons and daughters, young and old, servants, men and women (Acts 2:16-18).

This does not mean that all Christians will exercise the gift of prophecy as it is described in 1 Corinthians 12-14 or that they will be prophets in the Ephesians 4:11 sense, but it does mean that God has made his Spirit available to all so that we can all speak on his behalf. As we've already seen, Acts 8:1 tells us how, because of the persecution that had broken out against the church in Jerusalem, all the Christians (except the apostles) were scattered throughout Judea and Samaria. Verse 4 tells us that these people preached the word wherever they went. As a result, many people turned to Christ and the great church at Antioch was founded (Acts 11:19-21).

These people were not called to be 'preachers' in the way we tend to use the word today, nor were they prophets like John the Baptist, but they had received God's Spirit and they did speak out on his behalf, and in that sense they were both preachers and prophets! In short, all God's people are called to speak up for him. All God's people are prophets.

The gift of prophecy

In 1 Corinthians 12:8-11 Paul lists nine spiritual gifts. One of these is prophecy. 1 Corinthians 12:10-11 says:

> ...to **another** prophecy... he (the Spirit) gives them to each person just as he determines.

This strongly suggests that this gift is not given to everybody and Romans 12:6 backs this up by saying:

> We have **different** gifts according to the grace given us. **If a** man's gift is prophesying, let him use it in proportion to his faith.

This gift is given by the Spirit to individual Christians to speak words of encouragement and edification to the church. In 1 Corinthians 14:1-5 we read:

> 1. Follow the way of love and eagerly desire spiritual gifts, especially the gift of prophecy.

> 2. For anyone who speaks in a tongue does not speak to men but to God. Indeed, no one understands him; he utters mysteries with his spirit.

> 3. But everyone who prophesies speaks to men for their strengthening, encouragement and comfort.

> 4. He who speaks in a tongue edifies himself, but he who prophesies edifies the church.

> 5. I would like every one of you to speak in tongues, but I would rather have you prophesy. He who prophesies is

greater than one who speaks in tongues, unless he interprets, so that the church may be edified.

These verses make it very clear that the gift of prophecy is very valuable. The reason for this is that it edifies or builds up the church. It strengthens, encourages, and comforts God's people. In church it is more valuable than speaking in tongues because, although speaking in tongues edifies the person who is speaking, it doesn't help anyone else unless it's interpreted.

However, when an interpretation is given, speaking in tongues becomes just as valuable as prophecy. In fact, when speaking in tongues is understood, it is in itself a form of prophetic language. On the Day of Pentecost, when Peter was asked for an explanation of how the disciples were able to speak languages they had never learned, he replied that this was the fulfilment of Joel's prophecy that *your sons and your daughters shall prophesy* (Acts 2:17ff.).

All this shows us that God may speak to us through the gift of prophecy or through the interpretation of tongues[33] or even through speaking in tongues when the hearers understand the language that is being spoken, as on the Day of Pentecost. And I can testify from my own experience that God does speak to us in all these ways.

In 1959, when Eileen and I were seeking the baptism in the Holy Spirit, we decided that perhaps we should visit a Pentecostal Church to find out more and possibly ask for prayer. So one Tuesday evening we went to Bethel Church, Dagenham, when they were having their weekly prayer meeting. The church was several miles from where we lived and no one in the church had any idea of who we were. We

---

[33] For discussion of the view that interpretation should always take the form of praise, see *Body Builders*, pp. 126-129.

122

were slightly nervous as neither of us had ever been to a Pentecostal prayer meeting before and we didn't know what to expect. Would there be speaking in tongues, for example?

As it turned out, the meeting was not unlike the Baptist prayer meetings we were used to, apart from the fact that there were no real gaps between one person praying and the next. Then, just as we were getting used to it, somebody spoke in tongues. This was followed by an interpretation, which, to our total amazement, began with the words, *You have come into this church seeking to be filled with the Spirit...*

This was followed by two more 'messages' in tongues, each followed by an interpretation and we knew without a doubt that God was speaking directly to us. We continued to attend that Pentecostal prayer meeting and a few weeks later we were both baptised in the Holy Spirit and began to speak in tongues ourselves. This experience brought us into an entirely new dimension of Christian living and ever since we have been grateful for words from the Lord that have come either through prophecy or the interpretation of tongues.

Some years later, when I was pastoring a church in Basingstoke, we were both rather concerned when Eileen discovered that she had a lump in her breast. Fearing the worst but hoping for the best, we committed the matter to the Lord. We have always believed in divine healing, but we also believe that God expects us to take what medical help might be available[34], we weren't sure which was the right course of action in this case. So on Saturday night I asked the Lord to speak to us through the gifts of the Spirit in church the next morning.

---

[34]Please see *Just a Taste of Heaven* Chapter Sixteen for more details on why we should believe that medical treatment is one of the ways God uses to heal us.

And, sure enough, the answer came through an interpretation and a prophecy. After one person had spoken in tongues, someone else gave the interpretation:

> *You have considered the help of man, and that is great, but in this situation it is the Lord himself who will meet your need...*

At this point I began to cry and the floor was wet with my tears, when the interpretation was followed immediately by a prophecy: *For has he not promised to heal you...?!* Needless to say, the lump disappeared within days.

So God undoubtedly speaks to us through gifts like prophecy and the interpretation of tongues, but on rare occasions he speaks through the gift of tongues itself. This happened on the Day of Pentecost when people from several different nations heard the disciples speaking in their languages, and it still happens today.

One evening, some years ago, when I was Principal at Mattersey Hall Bible College, I was preaching in Newark when, in the middle of my message I spoke a few words in tongues. My purpose in doing so was to demonstrate that, when God has given us this gift, we can use it as a means of praying with our spirit whenever we wish (1 Corinthians 14:14-15).

Straight after the meeting, a woman with her husband approached me and said:

> *I'm rather embarrassed to speak with you, but, you see, I understood what you said when you spoke in tongues.*

Then she went on to explain that, although she had been a Christian for several years, she had never been able to give up smoking. Only that day her husband had said to her,

You really must give it up. If you don't, it will kill you.

She had replied, *I know, but it's so hard.*

She then went on to tell me that she and her husband were gypsies and that they had a language of their own known as Romany. I had never heard of such a language, yet when I spoke in tongues on that occasion, Romany was the language I was speaking. And what did it mean?

I have told you already. Cigarettes are not good for you!

So God has wonderful ways of speaking to us, through tongues or interpretation or through prophecy. And he also speaks through the ministry of prophets.

The ministry of a prophet

From what we've said so far, it should be clear that although all Christians are to 'prophesy' in the general sense of speaking on God's behalf, not all will exercise the gift of prophecy. And not all who exercise this gift will be prophets in the Ephesians 4:11 sense. In short:

- All God's people should prophesy (speak on his behalf)

- Some, but not all will receive the spiritual gift of prophecy (to edify the church)

- Some, but not all of these will exercise the ministry of a prophet.

So what can we learn about prophets as distinct from those who have the gift of prophecy? We saw earlier that prophets are people who hear from God and then pass on to others what he has said.

125

They speak on behalf of God. Of course, because God knows the future, prophets may foretell the future (if that is what the Lord reveals to them), but most of the time they speak on God's behalf to the people of their own generation. This was true of the prophets in the Old Testament and it's true of prophets today. However, there's a very important difference between prophets today and those of the Old Testament.

Differences between OT prophets and prophets today

Prophets today do not fulfil the same role as OT prophets and we should not expect them to do so. People like Moses, Elijah, Isaiah, Jeremiah, Ezekiel etc. were people of great power and influence, proclaiming God's word and manifesting his power to Israel and to the nations beyond[35]. But we must be careful not to assume that prophets today will be the same.

For a model of what we should expect of a prophet today we need to look at the New Testament and those who are described as prophets after the Day of Pentecost (Acts 2). Until then the Holy Spirit was given to relatively few people, but at Pentecost Moses' prayer that all God's people would be prophets (Numbers 11:29) was answered, and Joel's prophecy that God would pour out his Spirit on all people began to be fulfilled (Joel 2:28, Acts 2:16-17).

This meant that Acts 2 was in a very real sense a turning point in human history. The real dividing-line in God's dealings with mankind is not the break between Old and New Testaments, but the seven weeks that started with Christ's death and resurrection and that culminated with the outpouring of the Spirit at Pentecost. From then

---

[35] For other types of OT prophets, see *Body Builders*, Chapter 3.

on the Holy Spirit was available to all and, as we have seen, all God's people are in a sense 'prophets' (Acts 2:16-18).

This means that people referred to as prophets in the New Testament before Pentecost should be considered in the same category as the Old Testament prophets. John the Baptist, for example, was the last in the line of Old Testament prophets. Jesus himself made this clear when he said:

> For all the Prophets and the Law prophesied until John (Matthew 11:13).

In saying this Jesus revealed the continuity of the prophetic line from Moses right through to John for, until Jesus came, all prophetic ministry pointed forward to him.

But what was the purpose of prophetic ministry after Jesus had come? There clearly was to be a change of emphasis and we must not be surprised if certain differences appear in the role of the prophet after Pentecost. So, what is the ministry of a prophet today and how is it different from that of the Old Testament prophets?

To answer this question, we need to look at some of the people who are named as prophets in the Book of Acts[36]. These are Agabus (Acts 11:27-28, 21:10), Judas and Silas (Acts 15:32), and some or all of those mentioned in Acts 13:1-2 (Barnabas, Simeon, Lucius, Manaen, Paul). The difficulty here is that it is not clear whether they were all

---

[36] Anna (Luke 2:36), John the Baptist (Matthew 11:9), and the Lord Jesus (John 4:19), all exercised their ministry before Pentecost. Although the epistles mention certain OT prophets they refer to no post-Pentecost prophet by name. This means that the only examples of Ephesians 4:11 prophets named in the NT are to be found in Acts.

'prophets and teachers' or whether some were prophets and some were teachers.

Of all those mentioned in the previous paragraph, we know nothing more of Simeon, Lucius, Manaen, and Judas. Barnabas and Paul were also apostles and so it is difficult to distinguish their apostolic ministry from their prophetic ministry. Silas *said much to encourage and strengthen the brothers* (Acts 15:32) and preached that Jesus was the Christ, the Son of God (2 Cor.1:19-20). We know little else of his ministry except that he accompanied Paul on his second missionary journey[37].

This leaves Agabus of whom we know rather more. He clearly spoke with great revelation from the Spirit (Acts 11:27-28, 21:10) including the accurate prediction of certain future events. His prophecy about a widespread famine is a well-known example of this (Acts 11:27-30) as is his prediction of Paul's captivity in Jerusalem (Acts 21:11).

From this it is clear that his ministry involved more than the simple gift of prophecy which need not contain any element of prediction[38] However, there is no suggestion that he fulfilled a role similar to that of OT prophets like Moses, Elijah etc. who spoke prophetically to national leaders[39].

---

[37] For further discussion of Silas, see:
Kay, WK, *Prophecy*, Mattersey, Mattersey Hall, 1991, pp 38 & 45.

[38] See 1 Corinthians 14:3 which speaks of prophecy as 'strengthening, encouraging and comforting'. It does not mention prediction.

[39] Indeed, we must always remember that in the Old Testament God's people were a single nation, whereas in the New Testament the people of God are a multi-national church. After Pentecost there is no New Testament equivalent of a prophet speaking to a nation. Prophets speak to the church, for the church is now the people of God.

This leads me to the conclusion that though the prophets referred to in Ephesians 4:11 exercised a greater ministry than the simple gift of prophecy, they are by no means the same as the prophets of the Old Testament or as John the Baptist in the New. And that understanding must surely influence any conclusion we may wish to draw about the role of prophets today.

Prophets today – Agabus as an example
So to discover the role of prophets today, we must examine any NT examples of the ministry of prophets after Pentecost - and we have noted that Agabus is the only clear example.

We find references to the ministry of Agabus first in Acts 11 and then later in Acts 21. In Acts 11:27-28 we read that some prophets came to Antioch. One of them, named Agabus

> *stood up and predicted that a severe famine would spread over the entire Roman world.*

We are then told not only that this came to pass (v.28), but also what the disciples decided to do about it and how they did it. They decided that they would provide help for the brothers living in Judea (v.29) and they did so by sending a gift by Barnabas and Saul (v.30).

Two things are important here. First, Agabus' prediction came to pass. If it had not done so it would have been a false prophecy according to the principles laid down in Deuteronomy 18:21-22. Clearly if a prophetic revelation comes from God it will come to pass[40].

---

[40]In saying this, we need to remember that some prophecies have conditions attached. And some conditions are silent or 'understood'. For example, in Jonah 3:3 Jonah prophesied, *Forty days from now Niniveh will be*

Secondly, it is noteworthy that *the prophet did not tell the disciples what to do.* Agabus simply gave them information as to what would happen. There is no suggestion here, therefore, that the prophet gives direction to the church or to individuals. But this is something which becomes even clearer when we consider the later passage in Acts 21 where we read:

> ... *a prophet named Agabus came down from Judea. Coming over to us he took Paul's belt, tied his own hands and feet with it and said, "The Holy Spirit says, 'In this way the Jews of Jerusalem will bind the owner of this belt and will hand him over to the Gentiles' (vv.10-11).*

The disciples then pleaded with Paul not to go to Jerusalem (v.12), but Paul answered that if needs be he was ready to die in Jerusalem for the name of the Lord Jesus (v.13). Seeing that they could not persuade him, the disciples replied, *The Lord's will be done* (v.14).

Again we see clearly that *the prophet does not give direction* to Paul. Agabus tells Paul that he will go to Jerusalem and that he will be captured by the Jews and handed over to the Gentiles. He does not tell him not to go. It is the disciples in the following verses who plead with Paul not to go. They put their own interpretation on the prophecy. But Paul knew that they were misunderstanding what God was saying, for he himself knew what God wanted him to do.

To help us understand this we need to go back to Acts 20. Paul is on his way to Jerusalem, hoping to get there in time for the feast of

---

destroyed. But it wasn't, because the people repented. So was Jonah's prophecy false? No, there was a silent condition attached – unless the people repent. Compare Jeremiah 18:8-10.

Pentecost (v.16). He reaches Miletus and sends to Ephesus for the elders of the church (v.17). In his farewell address to them he says

> *And now, compelled by the Spirit, I am going to Jerusalem, not knowing what will happen to me there. I only know that in every city the Holy Spirit warns me that prison and hardships are facing me. However, I consider my life worth nothing to me, if only I may finish the race and complete the task the Lord Jesus has given me... (Acts 20: 22-24)*

Three things are significant here. First, it is clear that prophetic ministry was common at that time. *In every city* Paul was receiving prophetic words. Secondly, these prophetic words were testifying to the same thing. Paul would be imprisoned in Jerusalem. Thirdly, despite all this Paul was convinced that God wanted him to go for he was *compelled by the Spirit* to do so.

It is very important to understand this when we come to Acts 21:4 which says that *through the Spirit* the disciples at Tyre *urged Paul not to go on to Jerusalem.* This apparently completely contradicts Paul's own statement that he was *compelled by the Spirit* to go (20:22). However, the passage about Agabus (vv. 10-14) sheds light on this. The disciples at Tyre made the same mistake as those at Caesarea. They received a revelation from the Spirit as to Paul's future imprisonment, but they wrongly understood that this meant that Paul was not to go.

So the ministry of Agabus teaches us that prophets today may receive revelation from the Holy Spirit with regard to the future. However, it is not their role to tell the church or individual Christians what to do. They do not give direction. They impart to us information from the Spirit which helps us decide in advance what to do (Acts 11) or may encourage us that we are still in the will of God even when we are called to pass though hardship and difficulty (Acts 20-21).

One example of a present-day prophet is César Castellanos. When I met him he was the leader of a church in Columbia which was at the time almost certainly one of the fastest growing churches in the world, with over 200,000 members. In 1998 he visited Britain and was the guest preacher at a conference I attended. At the end of a special late-night meeting where César had been speaking to about a dozen national Christian leaders, he prayed for each one of us in turn. When he came to me, instead of praying, he prophesied. His prophecy included the following statement:

> *This is what the Holy Spirit says: I will greatly anoint your pen and your writing will be a blessing to thousands and thousands of people.*

How was I to respond to such a wonderful prophecy? Let's see what the New Testament has to say about this and then ask how it applies to César's prophecy about me. It's very important, when we hear prophetic words of this kind, that we consider very carefully what has been said and judge it in the light of what the New Testament teaches.

How to respond to the ministry of prophets today
In 1 Corinthians 14:29 we're told to judge or weigh carefully what a prophet says. We must not automatically assume that everything a prophet says comes from the Lord. A prophet may well have received something from the Lord, but the way they express it may be influenced by their own interpretation of what the Lord has given them.

Remember the people in Acts 21 who were telling Paul not to go to Jerusalem? They had heard rightly from the Lord that Paul would suffer when he went to Jerusalem, but they put their own construction on it and told him not to go! There's a human element in every prophecy, even when it's given by divine inspiration.

So how do we weigh or judge a prophecy? It will greatly help if we ask ourselves questions like these:

- Is the prophecy in line with the principles of Scripture?

- Is the person who brought the prophecy reliable?

- Do we have an inner witness that this is from the Lord?

- Are there any other signs confirming the prophecy?

If the answers to these questions are positive, then it would be wise to ask the Lord what our next course of action might be, and perhaps to seek the advice of one or more of our church leaders. Do they have any conviction that this is what God is saying?

Other important questions you might ask are:

- Is there any indication of the timing of the fulfilment of the prophecy? We shouldn't automatically assume that it will happen immediately.

- As time passes, can we see definite signs that the prophecy is coming to pass?

Now, just by way of example, if I apply these principles to César's prophecy about myself, I can certainly see that:

- His prophecy was in line with the principles of Scripture

- The person who brought the prophecy was reliable

- I did have an inner witness that it was from the Lord. It was a confirmation of what I had already felt that God was saying to me. In the weeks leading up to that conference I had been feeling that God wanted me to give more time to writing. César's prophecy came as a wonderful confirmation

- The fact that he did not know me was in itself a good sign of its genuineness. César had never met me. He knew that I was a Christian leader, but he had no way of knowing that I was a writer.

- There was an almost immediate fulfilment and it continues to be fulfilled over 20 years later. Since that time, I have written several books which have been translated into a variety of different languages. They have certainly reached thousands already and I continue to receive messages of thanks from grateful readers.

In using this illustration, I have simply tried to highlight the fact that God does still speak through prophets today and to show how important it is to know how to evaluate what they say. In the final analysis, as the children of God it is our privilege to be led by God's Spirit and, although he may choose to speak to us through prophetic ministry, we, and we alone, can determine God's will for our lives. And it's because we have the Spirit that God sometimes speaks to us more directly, without any human intermediary, and that will be the subject of the next five chapters.

PART FOUR

GOD SPEAKS TO US DIRECTLY BY HIS SPIRIT

CHAPTER ELEVEN

An Audible Voice

The Bible is full of examples of God speaking very directly, often without any human involvement. Some of the ways he speaks like this include:

- an audible voice

- angels

- dreams and visions

- supernatural signs

- promptings – the voice within.

In the next five chapters we'll look at each of these in turn, starting with some biblical examples and then illustrating wherever possible from my own experience. I say 'wherever possible' because I can't honestly say that God has spoken to me in all of these ways. I have certainly never heard his audible voice.

There are many examples in the Bible where we read that the Lord spoke to someone, but it's not always clear how he spoke. Consider the example we looked at in Chapter 1. We looked at Acts 13:1-3 where we read that the Holy Spirit **said,**

> Set apart for me Barnabas and Saul for the work to which I have called them.

The Holy Spirit may well have spoken with an audible voice on this occasion, but it's just as likely that the spoke through one of the prophets who were present (v.1).

On other occasions, however, it's perfectly clear that God's voice was audible. To mention just a few examples:

Isaiah heard the voice of the Lord saying,

> *Whom shall I send and who will go for us?* (Isaiah 6:8).

When Ezekiel had a vision of the glory of the Lord,

> *he fell face down and heard the voice of one speaking (Ezekiel 1:28).*

At Jesus' baptism a voice from heaven said,

> *This is my Son, whom I love; with him I am well pleased* (Matthew 3:17).

On the road to Damascus, Paul had a vision of Jesus, fell to the ground, and heard a voice say to him,

> *Saul, Saul, why do you persecute me?*(Acts 9:4).

Peter heard God's voice while praying on the rooftop in Joppa (Acts 10:13-16).

And on the isle of Patmos John *heard a loud voice, the voice of the Lord, telling him to write* (Revelation 1:10-12).

All these examples make it perfectly clear that God sometimes speaks with an audible voice. To learn more about this, we'll take Samuel as an example from the Old Testament before turning to the examples we find in the Gospels and Acts.

Samuel

Hannah, Samuel's mother, had been unable to have children, which, in the culture in which she lived, caused other women to despise her. But she prayed fervently to the Lord and promised that if he would give her a son, she would dedicate him to the Lord's service. So, when Samuel was born in answer to Hannah's prayer, she took him to the temple where the boy ministered before the Lord under Eli the priest (1 Samuel 2:11).

In chapter 3 we read how one night, while Samuel was lying down, the Lord called him by name. Samuel, not knowing that it was the Lord, ran to Eli and said,

> Here I am. You called me.

But Eli replied,

> I did not call; go back and lie down.

This happened three times, and by then Eli realised that it was God who was calling Samuel. He told him that, when the Lord called again, he should reply,

> Speak Lord, for your servant is listening.

When Samuel did so, the Lord spoke very clearly to him, and he was able to pass on to Eli what he had heard. It's evident that God's voice was audible on this occasion, because Samuel thought that it was Eli who was speaking. However, although it's very possible that God continued to speak to Samuel in the same way, this is something we can't be absolutely sure about. This was the beginning of Samuel's ministry as a prophet and, as we shall see, God often spoke very dramatically to people at the outset of their ministry.

Jesus' Baptism

Matthew, Mark, and Luke all record that after Jesus was baptised in the River Jordan, the Holy Spirit came on him and he heard God's voice speaking from heaven. In Mark and Luke it's clear that the words are spoken to Jesus himself:

> You are my Son, whom I love; with you I am well pleased (Mark 1:11. Luke 3:22).

In Matthew, however, the words are slightly different:

> This is my Son, whom I love; with him I am well pleased (Matthew 3:17).

The wording suggests that Matthew wants us to understand that God's voice was heard and understood, not only by Jesus, but also by John the Baptist, and possibly by any others who were present. Understood this way, God's intention can be seen as being:

- To assure Jesus of his divine Sonship and his Father's love

- To confirm to John the Baptist that Jesus is the Messiah

- To make clear to all present that, although Jesus was being baptised, he had no sins to confess[41].

This was a unique event in the life of Jesus and marked the beginning of his ministry (Luke 3:23). Immediately after it he was sent by the Spirit into the desert and was tempted by Satan (Mark 1:12-13).

---

[41] All the others came to be baptised, *confessing their sins* in preparation for the coming of the Messiah. Jesus was sinless and Jesus was the Messiah.

The Transfiguration of Jesus

The story of Jesus' transfiguration is recorded In Matthew 17:1-8, Mark 9:1-9, and Luke 9:28-35. Luke's account is a little more detailed and is summarised below:

Jesus takes Peter, John and James up onto a mountain to pray. As he is praying, the appearance of his face changes, and his clothes become as bright as a flash of lightning. Moses and Elijah appear in glorious splendour, talking with Jesus. They speak about his departure, which he's about to bring to fulfilment at Jerusalem.

Peter and his companions are very sleepy, but when they become fully awake, they see Jesus' glory and the two men standing with him. As the men are leaving, Peter says, "Master, it is good for us to be here. Let us put up three shelters – one for you, one for Moses and one for Elijah."

But while he's still speaking, a cloud appears and envelops them, and they're afraid. Then a voice comes from the cloud, saying,

> This is my Son, whom I have chosen; listen to him (Luke 9:35).

> This is my Son, whom I love; with him I am well pleased. Listen to him! (Matthew 17:5 and Mark 9:7).

The slight variation in Luke's account need not concern us here. What is most significant is the similarity. God declares that Jesus is his chosen, well-loved Son, with whom he is well pleased. But to whom is he speaking? To Peter, James and John. Note the repetition of **Listen to him!**

Once again, as we saw with regard to God's audible voice at Jesus' baptism, this is another unique event in the life of Jesus and it happens not only for the benefit of the three disciples who were present, but also for Christians ever since. Peter clearly saw it like that, because decades later he refers to it in 2 Peter 1:16-18 where he states:

> We did not follow cleverly invented stories when we told you about the power and coming of our Lord Jesus Christ, but we were eyewitnesses of his majesty.

> For he received honour and glory from God the Father when the voice came to him from the Majestic Glory, saying, "This is my Son, whom I love; with him I am well pleased."

> We ourselves heard this voice that came from heaven when we were with him on the sacred mountain.

And we see something similar in John 12:27-30, where we read:

> Now my heart is troubled, and what shall I say? 'Father, save me from this hour'? No, it was for this very reason I came to this hour. Father, glorify your name!" **Then a voice came from heaven,**

> **I have glorified it, and will glorify it again.**

> The crowd that was there and heard it said it had thundered; others said an angel had spoken to him. Jesus said,

> **This voice was for your benefit, not mine.**

So in the NT accounts that we've looked at so far in this chapter, it appears that God's purpose in speaking with an audible voice was largely, though not exclusively, **to demonstrate to others** exactly who Jesus was, and in so doing to strengthen their faith. But, as we now turn to examples in the Book of Acts, we see a rather different emphasis.

Paul's conversion

The story of Paul's conversion is found in Acts 9. He is on his way to Damascus in order to arrest any Christians he might find there. Then in verses 3-7 we read:

> As he neared Damascus on his journey, suddenly a light from heaven flashed around him. **He** fell to the ground and **heard a voice say to him,** "Saul, Saul, why do you persecute me?" "Who are you, Lord?" Saul asked. "I am Jesus, whom you are persecuting," he replied. "Now get up and go into the city, and you will be told what you must do." **The men traveling with Saul** stood there speechless; they **heard the sound but did not see anyone.**

It's clear from verses 4 and 7 that the voice was speaking to Paul and that, although his companions heard the sound of the voice, they did not understand it. This is confirmed in Acts 22:6-9 where Paul himself is telling the story:

> About noon as I came near Damascus, suddenly a bright light from heaven flashed around me. I fell to the ground and **heard a voice say to me,** 'Saul! Saul! Why do you persecute me?' "'Who are you, Lord?' I asked. "'I am Jesus of Nazareth, whom you are persecuting,' he replied. **My companions** saw the light, but **they did not understand the voice** of him who was speaking to me.

So, unlike the passages where God's audible voice is heard in the ministry of Jesus, and is largely for the benefit of others, in Paul's case the voice was speaking to Paul himself and not to anyone else. But this does not mean that this was to be the regular way God spoke to Paul. That's clear as we read on in the Book of Acts. This was a unique event which was to inaugurate the ministry of the man who was to become the apostle to the Gentiles. But that brings us to the experience of Peter on the rooftop in Joppa.

Peter at Joppa

In Acts 10:1-8 an angel appears in a dream to a Roman centurion called Cornelius and tells him to send for Peter who is staying in Joppa with Simon the tanner whose house is near the sea. So Cornelius sends a soldier and two of his servants to fetch Peter from Joppa.

Then, in verses 9-17 we read that as the men are on their journey the next day, Peter goes up on the roof to pray. There he falls into a trance and has a vision of a large sheet containing all kinds of animals, birds and reptiles. Then in verses 13-20 we read:

> Then *a voice told him*, "Get up, Peter. Kill and eat." "Surely not, Lord!" Peter replied. "I have never eaten anything impure or unclean." *The voice spoke to him a second time*, "Do not call anything impure that God has made clean." This happened three times, and immediately the sheet was taken back to heaven.
>
> While Peter was wondering about the meaning of the vision, the men sent by Cornelius found out where Simon's house was and stopped at the gate. They called out, asking if Simon who was known as Peter was staying there.
>
> While Peter was still thinking about the vision, *the Spirit said to him*, "Simon, three men are looking for you. So get up and

go downstairs. Do not hesitate to go with them, for I have sent them."

Without going into further detail, four things are noteworthy here:

- The voice Peter heard was part of a vision he was having

- Peter was the only person to hear the voice

- Peter's experience was a key turning point in the history of the Christian Church

- When the vision is over, God still speaks to Peter, but presumably not with an audible voice (see v.19).

So, bearing in mind what we've discovered in the passages we've been examining, it seems reasonable to draw the following conclusions:

- Speaking with an audible voice is not God's usual way of speaking to us

- When he does so, it is usually at a key turning point in our lives, inaugurating a new area of ministry

- He does speak to individuals in this way, but, especially in the case of Jesus, God's voice was collectively heard by others and was largely for their benefit.

In short, hearing God's audible voice is exceptional and we should not be disappointed if he does not speak to us in this way. Although God has spoken to me in many wonderful ways, I have never heard his audible voice and I know very few people who would claim to have done so. However, rather more frequently we hear of God speaking through the ministry of angels.

CHAPTER TWELVE

Angels

As far as I know, I have never seen an angel and have never heard an angel speak to me – although we need to remember that some people have shown hospitality to angels without knowing it (Hebrews 13:2). But both Old and New Testaments show that God sometimes speaks to his people through the ministry of angels.

The word angel comes directly from the Greek word *aggelos* (pronounced angelos) and simply means messenger. Angels are God's messengers. They are ministering spirits sent to serve those who will inherit salvation (Hebrews 1:14). A good example of this is when the angel Gabriel appeared to Zechariah, the father of John the Baptist and told him that his prayer had been heard and that his wife, Elizabeth, who was barren, would bear him a son. Humanly speaking, this was totally impossible because both Zechariah and Elizabeth were now far too old. I think Zechariah's question was quite understandable:

> *How can I be sure of this? I am an old man and my wife is well on in years* (Luke 1:18).

Gabriel's reply in the next verse illustrates perfectly the ministry of angels:

> *I am Gabriel. I stand in the presence of God, and have been sent to speak to you and tell you this good news* (Luke 1:19).

Angels are God's messengers. They stand in God's presence and are sent to speak to us[42]. The Gospels and Acts give us plenty of examples. About six months after his visit to Zechariah, God sent the angel Gabriel to Nazareth, to a virgin whose name was Mary (Luke 1:26-27). It was angels who brought the good news of Jesus' birth to the shepherds and told them where they would find him (Luke 2:8-14).

It was an angel that came from heaven and appeared to Jesus in the Garden of Gethsemane, strengthening him (Luke 22:43). And it was the angel of the Lord who descended from heaven and rolled away the stone from the mouth of Jesus' tomb and told the women who had come to anoint the body of Jesus that he was risen (Matthew 28:1:7).

In the Book of Acts, as the disciples were looking intently up into the sky, two men dressed in white stood beside them (Acts 1:10). They told them:

> This same Jesus who has been taken from you into Heaven, will come back in the same way as you have seen him go into Heaven (v,11)

These *men dressed in white* were undoubtedly angels[43] sent by God to remind them of Jesus' promise that he would come again (John 14:28).

---

[42] Note, incidentally, that we too are called to be God's messengers. We are to spend time in his presence, hear what he has to say, so that he can send us to others with the message of the good news of the gospel.

[43] Compare Mark 16:5 where the angel tells the women that Jesus has risen is described as a young man dressed in a white robe.

In Acts 5:19 the angel of the Lord opened the prison doors and released Peter and John. In Acts 8:26 an angel told Philip the evangelist to go south to the road that leads from Jerusalem to Gaza. This led to the conversion of a key national leader from the land of Ethiopia.

In Acts 10 it was an angel who spoke to both the apostle Peter and the Roman centurion Cornelius (verses 3, 7, 22) resulting in the conversion of Cornelius and his entire household. In Acts 12 it was the angel of the Lord who once again released Peter from prison (verses 7-11). And in Acts 27:23-24 it was an angel who stood beside Paul before the ship on which he was travelling was wrecked on the island of Malta and said:

> Do not be afraid, Paul. You must stand before Caesar, and God has graciously given you the lives of all who sail with you,

Now the Book of Acts was not written simply as a historical account of the beginnings of the early church. Most scholars are agreed that Luke's intentions in writing it were not merely historical. They are theological and missional. Luke is not just teaching us how it was, but how it can and should be[44]. And in recording the frequent activity of angels, he is surely telling us that we can at times expect angelic intervention too.

There have certainly been many anecdotal reports recently of people claiming to have experienced the presence of angels in one way or another and I see no good reason to doubt this, particularly when the testimony comes from a reliable source. As far as Eileen and I are concerned, although God has never spoken to us through an angelic

---

[44] See my comments on this in Chapter Five.

messenger, I am confident that we have experienced angelic help on at least one occasion.

In 1977 I served as Acting Principal of Mattersey Hall for six months before being appointed Principal in 1978. During that time we were still living in Basingstoke although I was at Mattersey much of the time about 200 miles away from home.

One weekend I went with about 50 of our students from Mattersey to Newport in South Wales. There was a big inter-church meeting on the Saturday night and on the Sunday the students went to different churches to sing, testify, and preach. I stayed in Newport to preach in the church there.

After Sunday lunch the pastor, Eric Dando, asked me if I would like to phone Eileen, which of course I was grateful to do. After telling her that the weekend was going well, I asked her how she was and was shocked to hear her reply.

I'm O.K., she said, *but I very nearly wasn't!*

Oh! What's happened? I replied.

And she told me what had happened to her on the Saturday night while I had been away preaching in Newport. There had been a women's missionary meeting in London and Eileen and several of the ladies from the church in Basingstoke had gone to it. They had travelled in two cars and on the way home, on the road between Reading and Basingstoke, several horses ran into the road in front of the cars. It seems that they had escaped from a nearby field.

One of the horses collided with the car in which Eileen was travelling in the front passenger seat. The impact was so great that the front of the car roof caved in to within an inch of Eileen's head. The car was a complete write-off and, as the people from the car in front walked back to see exactly what had happened, they feared the worst.

At this point it is important to explain that at that time the wearing of seat-belts was not compulsory in the U.K. and the car in which Eileen was travelling didn't have any. Bearing in mind the speed at which the car had been travelling when it collided with the horse, both Eileen and the driver should have been thrown forward through the windscreen. Indeed, the woman seated behind Eileen was thrown forward so violently into the back of Eileen's seat that it was twisted out of position.

Yet Eileen was not thrown forward, and none of those travelling in that car was seriously injured. They all walked away relatively unharmed. As she related the story afterwards Eileen told me that throughout the whole incident she was strangely conscious of something – or someone? – holding her to the back of her seat, preventing her from being thrown forward. Was it a coincidence that on that very evening I had been preaching in Newport on a subject I have rarely preached on before or since? My subject was ANGELS.

Of course, I cannot categorically state that Eileen was saved by an angel. But I am certain that Eileen's life was spared by divine intervention of some kind – and, as we have seen, the Bible does say that angels are messengers God sometimes sends to be of help to his people.

More recently I had an experience of answered prayer which several of my friends have suggested might have been brought about by angels. It was Sunday May 9th 2021 at around 10.45am. I was travelling from Brixham, where we live, to Newton Abbot for a COVID test. This was required because I was due to go into hospital on the Tuesday for an exploratory procedure on my larynx. If I tested positive for COVID I would not be allowed into hospital for the operation.

Shortly after I started my journey I noticed a gentle banging sound coming from the rear of the car. At first I wasn't too concerned and anyway I didn't want to stop as I didn't want to miss the appointment for the COVID test which was at 11am. If I had missed the appointment the procedure would have had to be postponed. So I continued my journey hoping that the banging was nothing serious,

Within a few miles, however, the banging had become much louder and I was getting scared. Finally, in desperation I called out, *Lord Jesus, please take care of this!* Seconds later I saw in the mirror a car behind me flashing its headlights. It drew alongside me and indicated that I needed to pull over into the layby that was about fifty yards ahead.

When I did so the problem was obvious. My nearside back wheel was coming off! Two of the five nuts that hold the wheel on were missing and the other three were loose. If I had continued like that, the consequences could have been fatal. Relieved that the other driver had pulled me over in time, I asked if he could help me, explaining the urgency of getting to the COVID appointment. This he gladly did and, when he searched in the boot for the wheel brace, he discovered that there were two spare wheel nuts there! It took less than a minute for him to fix the wheel and he was on his way. And I reached Newton Abbot just in time for my appointment. I think I have never known such a quick and dramatic answer to prayer.

Now, of course, I cannot be sure that the man who fixed my wheel was in fact an angel, but I'm open to that possibility. But in a way it really doesn't matter. What matters is that the Lord answered my prayer, saved my life and brought me safely through the operation. Whether or not he used an angel to do so is unimportant. As we have seen, the Bible does tell us that angels are God's messengers and that they are sent to minister to God's people. I believe it because the Bible says so, not because I've had an experience that may or may not have involved an angel.

CHAPTER THIRTEEN

Dreams and visions

I guess most Christians know that the Bible contains many references to God speaking to people through a dream or vision. The book of Genesis alone contains some 40 references to the word dream, and at least seven people are mentioned as having been spoken to in a dream or vision. These include:

- Abimelech (20: 3, 6)

- Abraham (15:1)[45]

- Jacob (31: 10, 11)

- Laban (31: 24)

- Joseph (37: 5, 6, 9, 10)

- Pharaoh's Butler and Baker (40: 5, 8, 9, 16)

- Pharaoh (41: 7, 8, 15, 17, 22, 25, 26, 32).

And in the rest of the Old Testament there are many other references too, far too many to mention here. The most significant of these is Joel's prophecy:

> *And afterwards, I will pour out my Spirit on all people. Your sons and daughters will prophesy, your old men will dream dreams, your young men will see visions...* (Joel 2:28),

---

[45] This is the only reference to the word *vision* in Genesis. All the other references in the list are to dreams.

We'll return to this when we come to look at dreams and visions in the New Testament, but first let's consider three other OT passages. The first is in the book of Job which is considered to be the oldest of all the books of the Bible and in it we find Elihu saying to Job:

> Why do you complain to God that he responds to no one's words? For God does speak - now one way, now another - though no one perceives it. In a **dream**, in a **vision** of the night, when deep sleep falls on people as they slumber in their beds, he may speak in their ears... (Job 33:13-16).

Now it's important when reading Job to be aware that not everything Job's friends said to him was correct, but in this case Elihu's words are in line with what God himself says in Numbers 12:6-8:

> When there is a prophet among you, I, the Lord, reveal myself to them in **visions**, I speak to them in **dreams**. But this is not true of my servant Moses; he is faithful in all my house. With him I speak face to face, clearly and not in riddles; he sees the form of the Lord.

Here God confirms that he does speak through dreams and visions, but also makes it clear that they are 'riddles' and can be open to misinterpretation. They are not as reliable as the level of revelation that God granted to Moses. They need to be interpreted, as we know from the well-known stories of Joseph and Daniel who were gifted by God in interpreting dreams.

Finally, in Jeremiah 23 we are warned against the danger of false visions:

> This is what the Lord Almighty says: Do not listen to what the prophets are prophesying to you; they will fill you with false

hopes. They speak visions from their own minds, not from the mouth of the Lord (v.16. Compare 14:14).

Let the prophet who has a dream recount the dream but let the one who has my word speak it faithfully for what has straw to do with grain? declares the Lord (v.28).

The context here is that God had told Jeremiah that judgment was coming on the nation, but this, of course, was an unpopular message that nobody wanted to believe. The false prophets, who were politically motivated, were only saying what they knew the king wanted to hear. Through Jeremiah God is warning these prophets to make sure that they are speaking God's word faithfully and not prophesying visions from their own minds. And he is warning those who are listening to them not to believe them.

So the OT passages we have been looking at teach us that:

1. We sometimes think that God does not respond to us, but he does in one way or another, sometimes by a dream or vision (Job 33:13-16).

2. Even when God does speak through a dream or vision, it often needs to be interpreted (Numbers 12:6-8)[46].

3. Visions and dreams need to be evaluated. What is the motivation of the person relating their dream? Are they faithful to God's word? (Jeremiah 23:16, 28).

4. As we see from the example of faithful Moses, there is a higher level of revelation than dreams and visions. For us,

---

[46] Although rather different, compare the need for speaking in tongues to be interpreted – 1 Corinthians 14:1-5.

that is the teaching of Scripture. This is in harmony with what we have already seen with regard to different levels of prophecy[47].

As we come now to look at the New Testament, we see that here too there are frequent references to God speaking through dreams and visions. In the Gospels we read about Joseph and the wise men in the Christmas story, and Pilate's wife having dreams, and of Zechariah, Peter, James, and John having visions[48]. In Acts, God (or an angel sent by God) speaks in visions to Cornelius, Peter, and Paul[49].

The references in Acts are particularly important for us, because, as we have explained before, we are living after Pentecost which was a turning point in human history[50]. The gift of God's Holy Spirit was then made available to all his people. When the crowd, composed of many different nationalities, are amazed to hear the disciples speaking their languages, they ask, *What does this mean?* To which Peter replies:

> *...this is what was spoken by the prophet Joel:*
>
> *'In the last days, God says, I will pour out my Spirit on all people. Your sons and daughters will prophesy, your young men will see **visions**, your old men will dream **dreams**. Even on my servants, both men and women, I will pour out my Spirit in those days, and they will prophesy...* (Acts 2:16-18).

---

[47] See Chapter Ten
[48] Matthew 1:20, 2:12, 19, 22; Matthew 2:12; Matthew 27:19; Luke 1:22; Matthew 17:9
[49] Acts 10:3; Acts 10:17-19; Acts 16:9-10, 18:9, 26:19 (referring to Damascus Road)
[50] See pages 11-13

This seems to suggest that, far from any idea that dreams and visions might become redundant after Pentecost, there should in fact be an increase in these manifestations. They are a direct result of the Spirit being made available to all. What's more, if God spoke to Cornelius, Peter, and Paul through visions, there is no reason to suppose that he will not speak in the same way to people today, And indeed, there are increasing numbers of testimonies of Muslims around the world who have come to Christ as a result of God speaking to them through a dream or vision[51].

Finally, before I share a personal testimony of how God spoke to me in a dream, it's worth noting that in Acts 2 Peter identifies the manifestation of speaking in tongues as the fulfilment of Joel's prophecy that when the Spirit was poured out in the last days all kinds of people would see dreams and visions and that they would prophesy.

This may well suggest that, just as dreams and visions are a means of prophetic revelation, speaking in tongues fulfils a similar role. It certainly did so on the Day of Pentecost and, as we have seen, when accompanied by the gift of interpretation of tongues, it can be a means of building up believers in the local church[52]. God has spoken to me many times through these gifts, but only once has he spoken to me through a dream.

Some years ago, my daughter, Sarah, recommended a book by Jack Deere entitled, *Surprised by the Voice of God*. On reading it, I was challenged by the reminder that in the Bible God often spoke through dreams, and I wondered why God had never spoken to me in a dream. So I said, almost casually,

---

[51] See, for example, *A Wind in the House of Islam* by David Garrison.
[52] See 1 Corinthians 14 and pages 121-126.

Lord, you have never spoken to me in a dream, and I would really like you to.

I must admit that I didn't expect an immediate answer, but a few days later I had a dream. But before I tell you what it was, I need to tell you about our family. Debbie, our oldest daughter was living in Rugby. Sarah, our second daughter, was living in Portsmouth. And Jonathan, our son, was living near Liverpool.

About a year before I had the dream, Sarah had asked me if I knew anyone who needed a car. She had tried to sell her old one, but was offered only £300 for it and felt that she'd rather give it away than sell it for such a low price. I told her that I thought Jonathan would be grateful for it, and so she gave the car to him.

Shortly before I had the dream, we had arranged to visit Debbie on a particular weekend and we knew that Jonathan would be there too. Now I had the dream about a week before the visit to Debbie. In my dream Eileen and I went to Debbie in separate cars because we would need to give Eileen's car to Jonathan. That was it. And even though I had asked the Lord to speak to me through a dream, I didn't seriously think that the dream was a message from God. And so we both went to Debbie's in my car.

Imagine my surprise when we arrived at Debbie's and saw what looked like a brand-new car standing outside Debbie's house.

Whose is the car? I said. To which Jonathan replied:

Oh, it belongs to the insurance company. Mine is a write-off. Someone smashed into the back of it while it was parked on the road.

And it was then that I was reminded of my dream. Could God be saying that we should give Eileen's car to Jonathan? I told her about the dream, and she readily agreed that that is what we should do. So we told Jonathan and simply asked that he would give us the insurance money when it came through, to put towards replacing the car we were giving him. We didn't expect very much as the most Sarah had been offered for it a year before was £300.

Eileen and I agreed together that we'd leave it a few weeks and then start to look for a replacement car for her. The car she had given Jonathan was a Toyota Corolla 1600, five door executive automatic, and Eileen loved it! So I promised her that we'd look for a newer version of exactly the same model. Shortly afterwards we heard from Jonathan. The insurance company had given him £1200 for the car, for which, if you remember, a year before Sarah had been offered a mere £300.

Grateful to God that we were getting far more than we had expected, Eileen and I set off one Saturday visiting car sales companies in several nearby towns, looking for a Toyota Corolla with the same specification. There was no such thing as on line shopping back then and it was pouring with rain all day long. After several hours of unsuccessful searching we returned home, tired, wet, and rather discouraged.

Then, quite suddenly, on the following Tuesday, a thought came into my mind. A few years earlier the College had bought a Toyota minibus from a Christian brother in Nottingham who had a garage with a Toyota franchise. Maybe I should try him? So I phoned him and told him what I was looking for. If he had one come in, would he please let us know? To which he replied, *Will silver do?*

Now the colour of the car was about the only detail I hadn't specified when I told him what we were looking for, but silver was just the sort of colour we wanted!

Yes, that's fine, I said. *Does that mean you've got one?*

And to cut a long story short, one had come in that very day. There was just one previous owner and they had only covered 3000 miles a year from new. The price was right, and when he said,

> *When do you want to come over and look at it?*

my reply was,

> *I don't need to. This is so obviously God, I'll come and get it on Saturday.*

That's the only time I've ever bought a car without looking at it, and it was just what Eileen wanted.

Now you may think that I've wandered a long way from the dream I was telling you about, but if it had not been for that dream, that whole series of amazing events would never have happened. And the story is not just about a dream about a car. It's a testimony of how God is at work in the little details of our lives, constantly working all things together for our good because he loves us and because we are called according to his purpose (Romans 8:28).

CHAPTER FOURTEEN

Supernatural signs

Another way God speaks to us is by supernatural signs. In Acts 2:22 Peter refers to Jesus as *a man accredited by God to you by miracles, wonders, and signs.* And in Hebrews 2:4 we read that God testifies to our salvation *by signs, wonders and various miracles, and gifts of the Holy Spirit.*

These three words, *miracles, signs,* and *wonders*, reveal three different aspects of the miraculous power of God. The word that is often translated as *miracle* literally means *power.* Miracles demonstrate how powerful God is, and they make us *wonder.* They cause amazement. They are also *signs.* They point the way.

As we look at both the Old and New Testaments, we see that through signs and wonders God is speaking to us, demonstrating his power, revealing his love, confirming his promises, and giving us direction. Perhaps the best OT example of God giving direction through supernatural signs is found in the story of Gideon (Judges 6-7). In these chapters God speaks to Gideon in several different ways:

- through a prophet (v8)
- by an angel (v12)
- by supernatural signs (vv17-21, 36-40)
- by speaking to him (possibly in a dream or vision) in the night (v25, 7:2, 4, 5, 7, 9)[53]
- through another person's dream and its interpretation (7:7-14)

---

[53] In none of these verses are we told *how* God spoke to him.

So supernatural signs are just one of several ways in which God speaks to Gideon, and, as we shall see, the signs God gives him are not so much a case of God speaking to him as a confirmation of what God has already said to him. But let's remind ourselves of the story.

The Israelites had done evil in the sight of the Lord and as a result were being oppressed by the Midianites. But when the Israelites cried out to the Lord for help, he sent a prophet who reminded them of how the Lord had delivered them in the past and told them the reason for their problem – they had not listened to the Lord. Then the angel of the Lord appeared to Gideon and said:

> *The Lord is with you, mighty warrior* (6:12).

When Gideon protests (v.13), the Lord says to him:

> *Go in the strength you have and save Israel out of Midian's hand. Am I not sending you?"* (v.14) *...I will be with you* (v.16).

Then Gideon says:

> *If now I have found favour in your eyes, **give me a sign** that it is really you talking to me* (v.17).

Gideon then brings an offering to the Lord and the Lord responds by touching it with the tip of his staff. Immediately fire flares up and consumes the offering and the angel disappears (v.21). Gideon, realising who he's been speaking to, fears for his life and says:

> *Ah, Sovereign LORD! I have seen the angel of the LORD face to face!"* (v.22).

But the Lord says to him:

> *Peace! Do not be afraid. You are not going to die* (23).

What's particularly noteworthy in this passage is the fact that Gideon seems to understand clearly the message he is receiving. God is with him and will use him to deliver Israel from the Midianites. But he needs reassurance because he finds it hard to believe that God would use someone like him and so he wonders if it really is God who is speaking to him (v17). So he asks for a sign.

Later in the chapter we read that the Spirit of the Lord came upon Gideon and that he blew a trumpet, summoning an army to follow him (vv.34-35). But, despite the promise and all the signs the Lord has already given him, Gideon still seeks reassurance and asks for further confirmation. In verses 36-40 we read:

> 36. Gideon said to God, "If you will save Israel by my hand as you have promised,
> 37. look, I will place a wool fleece on the threshing floor. If there is dew only on the fleece and all the ground is dry, then I will know that you will save Israel by my hand, as you said."
> 38. And that is what happened. Gideon rose early the next day; he squeezed the fleece and wrung out the dew – a bowlful of water.
> 39. Then Gideon said to God, "Do not be angry with me. Let me make just one more request. Allow me one more test with the fleece. This time make the fleece dry and the ground covered with dew."
> 40. That night God did so. Only the fleece was dry; all the ground was covered with dew.

Now it's important to understand this correctly, especially as some Christians today expect God to guide them by 'putting out a fleece'. They're not sure what God wants them to do, and so they say something like this:

Lord, if you want me to do A, let B happen.

Which is fine, if we understand that Gideon was asking God to do something that was supernatural, something which couldn't possibly happen unless *God* did it – like how God moved the shadow backwards for Hezekiah as a sign that he was extending his life for fifteen more years (2 Kings 20:1-11).

What's more, by asking God to make the fleece wet, and then dry, Gideon was not asking God to do something that might possibly be contrary to God's will. As an example of what I mean, consider the following. Let's suppose I want to know if God wants me to go to London tomorrow; so I say:

Lord, if you want me to go to London tomorrow, let my cousin John come and see me today.

I hope it's obvious that, although this fits the formula, *Lord, if you want me to do A, let B happen,* it's by no means an exact parallel with what Gideon did. Why do I say this? Because, although it might be unlikely that my cousin would come and see me today, and even if I might think that it would be a miracle if he did, it might just be God's will that my cousin does something completely different! So if God does want me to go to London tomorrow, but he doesn't want my cousin to come and see me today, how can he possibly answer the foolish prayer I've just prayed?!

So please be very careful about asking God to make something happen as a sign that he wants you to do something, especially as after the coming of the Spirit at Pentecost, there's no NT example of anyone 'putting out a fleece'.

Furthermore, it's worth remembering that Gideon shouldn't have needed this sign. God had already spoken very clearly to him in several ways and God's word should have been enough. Despite this, God graciously did what Gideon asked, as he does for us when, like Gideon, we need reassurance.

When we turn to the New Testament, we find that the main purpose of signs is to point people to Jesus. The star the wise men followed led them to Jesus (Matthew 2). Jesus himself performed signs and wonders because he knew that without them some people would not believe in him (John 4:48). The miracles he performed were signs that with the coming of Jesus the kingdom of God had come (Matthew 12:28, Luke 11:20). And Peter tells us that the miracles Jesus performed were signs that were given by God to testify who Jesus was (Acts 2:22).

As John is nearing the end of his Gospel, having recorded amazing miracles like Jesus turning water into wine, healing a man who was born blind, feeding five thousand people, and raising Lazarus from the dead, he writes:

> Jesus performed many other signs in the presence of his disciples which are not recorded in this book. But these are written that you may believe that Jesus is the Messiah, the Son of God, and that by believing you may have life in his name (John 20:30-31).

And God still works miracles to confirm the word of those who are preaching the good news about Jesus (Mark 16:15-20). This was the main purpose of the miracles recorded in the Book of Acts. Thousands came to faith in Jesus through the miracle of tongues at Pentecost (Acts 2:4) and the healing of the lame beggar in Acts 3 led to thousands more (Acts 4:4). In Acts 5 more and more men and women believed in the Lord as a result of the signs and wonders performed by the apostles (vv12-14). And when Philip the evangelist went to Samaria, crowds of people saw the signs he performed, believed in Jesus and were baptised (Acts 8:6-7, 12).

So the main purpose of signs in the New Testament was to point people to Jesus. But how does this help us if we're already Christians? How does God speak to us through signs? Part of the answer is simply that miraculous signs encourage our faith. The passage in John that we just referred to can also be translated *that you may* **continue** *to believe.*

And who can deny that testimonies of miracles today encourage the faith of believers? Since the publication of my book, *Signs from Heaven – why I believe,* in which I record some of the miracles I have seen in my own life and ministry, people have told me how much it has encouraged their faith. But that leads me to an experience which I shared in that book and how it radically altered the direction of my life.

You may remember that in Chapter Six of this book I told you of the impact Laurie Dixon had made on my life. Remember the story of the falling rock that just missed me on the mountainside in Switzerland and how that led to Laurie telling me about the baptism in the Holy Spirit?   That was in 1958. Now fast forward to July 1959.

Eileen, who was then my girlfriend, and I were sitting in the youth meeting at church singing from a well-known chorus book, when I happened to notice a list of books advertised on the back cover, one of which was entitled, *The full blessing of Pentecost*, by Dr Andrew Murray. Immediately I concluded that this book must be dealing with the subject Laurie had been talking about last year in Switzerland, and I suggested that it might be good to get it. In a few days, Eileen received a reply from the advertisers saying that the book was no longer available.

A bit disappointed, I returned home from Eileen's to my parents' house for lunch. As the meal was not quite ready, I went into the sitting room to wait. On entering, I happened to notice a book lying on the piano and casually picked it up - *The full blessing of Pentecost* by Dr Andrew Murray! But how did it get there? No one, except Eileen, knew anything of my interest in the subject. My parents did not know where the book had come from. It is true that my father had always had a large collection of books, but if it was his, he certainly had never read it, and didn't even know that he possessed it. Anyway, why wasn't it in the bookcase and how did it get on the piano?

No one to this day has any idea how that book came to be there on the very day that I had thought it to be unobtainable. The answer must surely lie in the realm of the supernatural – maybe an angel? But even if you think up a natural explanation – and that's always possible for those who don't want to believe – how likely is it that this was just a coincidence? No, God was confirming to us that we needed to be baptised in the Spirit, and when we had read the book, and were persuaded that the experience was biblical, we were both baptised in the Spirit and began to speak in tongues.

Of course, as I mentioned in the last paragraph, those who are sceptical try to explain away such things as the appearance of the book as coincidences. Indeed, all answers to prayer tend to be dismissed in that way. But, as a former archbishop of Canterbury once said, I find that when I pray, coincidences happen. When I don't pray, they don't!

In fact, what at first sight might appear to be a coincidence may very well turn out to be a sign. When one 'coincidence' happens after another, we may very well conclude that what is happening is actually the activity of God. This is how God spoke to me when I desperately needed to be sure that the pathway we had embarked upon was really in the will of God.

It was at the beginning of the 1980s while I was Principal of Mattersey Hall Bible College. As the facilities at the time were, to say the least, outdated, and as the number of students was increasing rapidly, we urgently needed to provide new accommodation for them. It was estimated that we would need £600,000 to do this (which in today's terms would be more like £6 million). But we had nothing in the bank.

The matter was so serious that the Board of Governors referred it to the Executive Council, and the Executive Council referred it to the General Council of Assemblies of God meeting in its Annual General Conference in Minehead.

The matter was discussed at length and, during the course of the debate, one of the pastors went to the microphone and asked me a direct question:

David, have you heard from the Lord?

In all honesty I had to answer,

No, I just know that we need this new building.

The debate drew to a close and the matter was put to the vote. To my delight, the proposition to go ahead received the two-thirds majority required by the Constitution. Now all we needed was the money!

After the vote had been carried by so large a majority, I fully expected the money to come pouring in. But very little came! Everyone seemed to be leaving it to everyone else! As the time for the signing of the contract drew near, we still had very little money, and I began to be anxious. Who has to sign the contract? What happens if the money doesn't come in? Who goes to prison if the money doesn't come in?! These were serious questions that were troubling my mind, and I kept remembering the question that pastor had asked me in Minehead: *David, have you heard from the Lord?*

Eventually, in desperation I said to Eileen:

> *I need to hear from God about this. I'm going to pray all night, and if he doesn't speak to me, I'm going to phone the Board of Governors and cancel the whole thing.*

So I began my night of prayer. After several hours, at around 2am, I began to feel like giving up. God wasn't speaking and I really didn't know what to do. I decided to take a break, so I sat down on the settee and picked up a copy of *Redemption Tidings* magazine.

As I opened it the title on the editorial page struck me forcibly: FAITH. So I began to read. Now if you have ever been in desperate need to hear from God and have been in a meeting where someone has brought a prophetic word which you have known was just for you, you will understand just how I felt as I read that editorial. Every single word of it came as *Thus says the Lord* to David Petts. I knew that God had spoken. I knew that we were to go ahead. I knelt down by the

171

settee and sobbed into the cushion and asked God to forgive me for my lack of faith. Then I went to bed. From that moment I never doubted that God was behind our building project after all.

But that is not the end of the story. The next morning I went down to the College and walked into the office. Ernest Anderson, who was then a resident member of faculty, was standing there and I excitedly told him what had happened.

> *That's wonderful, David*, he said, *I was praying all night too.*

I thought it was strange that we had both decided independently to pray all night and I could not imagine why he had decided to do so.

> *Oh*, I said, *What were you praying for?*

To which he replied:

> *I was praying for the same thing. I knew that unless you, as the Principal of the College, heard from God, the thing would never happen.*

> *Oh, thank you Ernest*, I said, *but you could have gone to bed at 2 o'clock!*

I immediately telephoned Colin Whittaker, the editor of the magazine.

> *Colin*, I said, *you have written the greatest editorial you will ever write,*

and I told him what had happened. Then he told me that he had known when he was writing the editorial that he was writing it for the College, but he had not felt able to be that explicit in print.

Some coincidence! I knew beyond doubt that this was far more. That series of events could not possibly be coincidence and through it I received confirmation that what I had read really was a word from God, a word that gave me faith for something bigger than myself. And, of course, because it was from God, it came to pass.

But faith does not always see immediate results. It is sometimes tested, and in fact it was a few years before the building was finally complete. There was an initial response as I told the story of how the Lord has spoken to me, and we were soon able to provide new accommodation for 32 of our students, but then the flow of funds dried up and building had to be delayed. Sure that we had received a word from the Lord, the Board of Governors, of which I was a member, decided to spend a day together in prayer and fasting.

Towards the end of the day, Paul Newberry shared with us two verses that he felt the Holy Spirit had impressed upon him from Micah 7:

> *Do not gloat over me, my enemy! Though I have fallen, I will rise. Though I sit in darkness, the LORD will be my light (v8).*

> *The day for building your walls will come, the day for extending your boundaries (v11).*

It seemed to us that the Lord was saying that the enemy would have no reason to gloat over the present delay in our building project. Now was not God's time for more building development, but that the time for building would surely come.

Encouraged by this I went home. Our daughter Sarah was home from college and I called to her as I entered the house.

I'm up here, she said, calling from her bedroom.

I went up to see her and, to my surprise, she was sitting in the dark. When I asked her why, she replied in the words of Micah 7:8.

Though I sit in darkness, the Lord will be my light!

What a confirmation! The same verse from two different people in two different places in the space of less than one hour.

And, of course, the time for building did come, and at the time of preparing this chapter, I'll be back there teaching this week and I think I'll be staying in that very building.

But now it's time to summarise what we have learned in this chapter.

- Signs are not so much God *speaking* to us, but God *confirming* what he has said.

- Be careful if you're thinking of putting out a fleece.

- In the New Testament the main purpose of signs is to point people to Jesus. They also encourage the faith of those who are already Christians.

- With God there's no such thing as coincidence. He is working all things together for the good of those he has called according to his purpose. Remarkable coincidences are very often God's way of confirming what he's already said.

CHAPTER FIFTEEN

Promptings – the voice within

So far in Part Four we've been talking about ways in which God speaks to us directly rather than through other people. We've considered how he may speak with an audible voice, or through angels, or by dreams and visions, or by supernatural signs. We now turn our attention to what are often called *promptings*, by which I mean the voice of God's Spirit inside us.

In John 14-16 Jesus told his disciples that he was going away, but that he would not leave them without help. He would send them another helper, the Holy Spirit, who would live within them (14:17) and would teach them, remind them of what he had said (14:26), guide them, and reveal to them things about the future (16:13).

And the same is true for us as his disciples today. Romans 8:11 tells us that God's Spirit lives within us and Galatians 4:6 says that, because we are his sons, God has sent the Spirit of his Son into our hearts. So we too can expect to hear the voice of God's Spirit inside us, teaching us, reminding us, guiding us, and even revealing things to us about the future.

Let me tell you about Hilda and Edna. They were both members of our church in Basingstoke. Edna had been saved as a teenager but had backslidden and married a man who was not a believer. Although she had come back to the Lord, she often struggled because of the problems caused by being 'unequally yoked' to an unbeliever (2 Corinthians 6:14).

Hilda was a widow who had come to Christ in her sixties during a mission I was conducting in our church. She lived in a council house which was only a few minutes' walk from a chip shop. One day, as she was walking across to the shop to get some fish and chips, a random thought came into her mind. *Go and see Edna.* She thought this might be from the Lord, but Edna lived over a mile away and if she went to see her the chip shop would be closed by the time she got back as the only means of getting to Edna was on foot. And anyway, she wasn't completely sure that the thought was from God, so she thought she might go and see Edna later.

But before Hilda had reached the chip shop the thought came again. *Go and see Edna NOW.* So she went. If the thought had come from God, she didn't want to disobey him. And when she arrived she knew, as soon as she saw Edna, that the thought had indeed come from God. Edna opened the door and burst into tears. She had been overwhelmed with the thought that nobody loved her, not even God. In desperation she had prayed,

> *Lord, if you really love me, please send someone to see me NOW.*

Hilda went without lunch that day, but what did that matter? She had been obedient to God and as a result had been a blessing to a fellow Christian who was struggling with her faith.

There's no doubt that Hilda's random thought was a prompting of the Holy Spirit. That's often how he speaks to us – by putting thoughts into our mind. But, of course, not every thought is a prompting of the Spirit and we need to learn how to distinguish the thoughts that come from him from those that don't. I'll be saying more about this later, but first let me give you a few examples from my own experience.

In the early 1970s, while I was pastoring at Basingstoke, I began to receive invitations to minister in other countries as well as in other churches up and down the UK. I was also teaching once a fortnight in our Bible College which was then at Kenley in Surrey. But there surely had to be a limit to how many invitations I could accept? I was expected to preach three times a week in the church I was pastoring.

One day, as I was praying about this, as if from nowhere the word *Antioch* came into my mind. Now I knew that Antioch was a place mentioned in the Book of Acts and that that was where the disciples were first called Christians (Acts 11:26). I also knew that Paul had set out from there on his first missionary journey, but I wasn't quite sure how this might be relevant to what I was praying about, so I decided to open my Bible and see what else I could discover about Antioch, and I very quickly came to Acts 13:1-3 where I read:

> *In the church at Antioch there were prophets and teachers: Barnabas, Simeon called Niger, Lucius of Cyrene, Manaen (who had been brought up with Herod the tetrarch) and Saul.*

> *While they were worshipping the Lord and fasting, the Holy Spirit said, "Set apart for me Barnabas and Saul for the work to which I have called them." So after they had fasted and prayed, they placed their hands on them and sent them off.*

Now Barnabas had been the first leader of the church at Antioch and he had brought Saul (or Paul) alongside him to help with the ministry (Acts 11:22-25). But now the Holy Spirit was telling them both to leave Antioch for a while and start on the church planting mission to which he had called them. But how could they leave Antioch? Who

177

would look after the church in their absence? The answer was simple. There were other prophets and teachers in the church (v1).

In giving me the word *Antioch* God was not only answering my question, but also showing me what was to become a key principle in the churches I have led, in the college at Mattersey Hall, and what I have since taught to church leaders around the world – the importance of team leadership[54].

It may be difficult to understand today, when team leadership is normal in many churches, but, in my experience, back in the seventies churches in most denominations were led by one man, who did all the preaching and led all the meetings. In giving me the word *Antioch* God was clearly telling me to look for other ministries in our church which would complement my own, give others an opportunity to exercise the gifts he had given them, and free me to accept invitations to minister elsewhere as he was leading me to an increasingly international ministry.

One example of this is how I came to visit several countries in Asia in 1986. It was on a Sunday in 1985. For no apparent reason the word *India* came into my mind. The impression was so strong that I said to Eileen,

I think the Lord is going to send me to India.

But I told no one else about it.

The following Wednesday evening Pastor Ray Belfield came to Mattersey to speak to the students about missions. After the meeting I invited him back to our house for a cup of tea before he made the

---

[54] For more on the biblical teaching on team leadership, please see *Body Builders*, Chapter Five.

journey back home to Wigan. As we prayed together before he left, I prayed that the Lord would show us more clearly how as a college we could do more about mission. As soon as I had finished speaking, Ray said to me,

I'll tell you what you can do. You can go to India.

This resulted in a month's trip the following January, not only to India, but also to Pakistan, Singapore, Malaysia and Indonesia. Ray's word was prophetic and came as a confirmation of what God had already begun to tell me the previous Sunday. It would have been a big decision to leave the college for a month if I had not had an excellent team of workers at Mattersey, plus the double assurance of what God wanted me to do – the inner voice of God's Spirit confirmed by a prophetic word.

And finally, let me tell you about Ruby. It was while I was leading the church in Basingstoke. We had invited an evangelist to come and conduct a series of special meetings. I encouraged the people to pray that God would give us one outstanding miracle of healing before the evangelist came and that this would attract people to the meetings.

So we began to pray months ahead of the evangelist's visit, which was to be in June. Then, on the Sunday after Easter, it happened! It was the evening service, and I was preaching about Thomas. He was the disciple who had been absent when Jesus, three days after he was crucified, appeared to his disciples on Easter Sunday. When the other disciples told Thomas that Jesus was alive, he simply refused to believe it. It was impossible! But a week later Jesus appeared to him too and showed him the wounds in his hands and feet. I remember saying something to the effect that the same Jesus whom Thomas had been able to see and touch was present with us right now even though we could not see him.

After the sermon, as we sang a closing song, a middle-aged woman walked – I should say *hobbled* – to the front of the church. This was a complete surprise to me as she had never been to our church before and I had not invited people to come forward for prayer, as we sometimes do. Neither had I mentioned healing. So I went to her and asked:

Can I help you?

She responded by saying:

If Jesus is present as you say He is, can He heal me **now**?

Immediately I *knew* that this was the miracle we had been praying for. It was as if God was saying, *This is it!*

He can, and he does! I said. *Be healed in the name of Jesus!*

And she RAN back down the aisle, instantaneously and completely healed. Ruby and her husband both became Christians and as a result of that miracle, a number of other people came to believe in Christ and became members of our church.

Now some people teach that we should always command healing in this way, but even Jesus only did what he saw his Father do (John 5:19). I will only command healing when I believe that's what God is telling me to do on that occasion. Otherwise, I believe we should *pray* for healing[55] rather than command it.

---

[55] For a more detailed explanation, please see *Just a Taste of Heaven - a biblical and balanced approach to God's healing power*.

So how do we know that that 'inner voice' is in fact the voice of God? If I've made it sound easy, I must admit that I haven't always found it so. Some people talk as though they're hearing words from the Lord all the time and I've sometimes thought, *I wish he'd talk to me like that!* I've also wondered if those people really are hearing the voice of the Lord as much as they think they are.

To help us get a better understanding about this we need to consider what the Bible has to say about where our thoughts come from, and as we do so we realise that some of our thoughts are not from God at all. They are temptations. The Bible shows us that in our Christian lives we are constantly fighting a battle against the world, the flesh, and the devil. Our thoughts are prompted by what we see, what we hear, and by the company we keep. So it's possible that a thought that we imagine has come from God could in fact be prompted by any of these things. So how can we be sure?

Bearing in mind what we've already said about how God speaks to us by Jesus, the word of God made flesh, and through the Bible, the written word, it goes without saying that any word he speaks by his Spirit in our hearts will always be in line with the character of Jesus and the principles of Scripture. If we are spending time with Jesus and meditating on his word, the thoughts that we have are more likely to come from God than if we spend most of our time watching television for example.

Another thing to consider is the kind of 'word' we feel the Lord might have given us. Is it a word of encouragement or is it giving us direction, or even telling us about the future? We'll consider each of these possibilities in turn, also taking into consideration whether we feel the word is for ourselves or someone else.

First, then, let's suppose an encouraging thought or verse of Scripture comes to your mind. We know from verses like 1 Corinthians 14:3 that part of the Spirit's role is to encourage us, so it would seem likely that the thought you've had has come from God. It might just be a line from a song that comes into your mind – something like, *The steadfast love of the Lord never ceases*, for example. Well, that's an easy one! It's totally in line with the teaching of the Bible, so, whether it's a prophetic word from the Spirit or not, it's true! So you can believe it and receive it, and pass it on to anyone who might need it.

But what about a thought or word where it seems that God is giving you direction, where he's telling you to do something? That's not quite so simple. Again, the first question to ask is, *Is it in line with Scripture?* The better you know your Bible, the better you'll be able to answer this question. Obviously, if it's contrary to Scripture, it isn't from the Lord.

But what if it is in line with Scripture, but you're not sure if it's for you? For example, let's suppose you get a feeling or thought that the Lord wants you to go to China and preach the gospel. That's certainly in line with Scripture, as Jesus has told us to make disciples of all nations. But we're not all called to China, and you'd need to be very sure that your thought or feeling really was from the Lord. In this case a single thought or feeling would not be enough. It needs to be confirmed. But how?

It seems that God has an infinite variety of ways of confirming his word to us. Much of this book has been about the many ways God spoke and confirmed his word to his people in the past and how he continues to do so today. These have included angelic visitations, dreams and visions, supernatural signs, and prophetic words. We have also mentioned persistent repetition and apparent coincidence, when a thought or word comes repeatedly from a variety of different sources, and we become convinced that it can only be God. To this we should add that, if the word you've received is as serious as being called to China, it would be wise to discuss it with your church leaders and see if they have any witness about it.

And the same guidelines hold good for a situation where you feel that God has revealed to you something about the future. It's important not to act upon it unless it's been confirmed in the sort of ways we've just mentioned. And if it involves someone else, it's vital that we have confirmation before we share it with them – and even then, it's always best to begin by saying something like this:

I feel that God has given me a word for you. If it's really from hm, I believe you will know in your heart that it's for you.

But even before we do that, it would be wise to search our own hearts by asking if the word is really for others or is it something that God is saying personally to us. This holds good not only when we feel the word we have is for a particular individual, but also when it comes during a meeting at church or in a home group.

The exercise of spiritual gifts like prophecy or interpretation of tongues is a separate subject, but learning how God speaks to us and discerning whether what he's saying is something for others or just for ourselves is clearly important if we believe that the Lord wants to use us in these gifts. In fact, I think that most of what I have learnt about recognising the inner voice of God's Spirit has been by using these gifts.

A good example is how I started to exercise the gift of interpretation of tongues. I first spoke in tongues when I was baptised in the Holy Spirit on September 8th, 1959, just four weeks before starting my studies at Brasenose College, Oxford. I enjoyed the meetings at the church I attended and soon began to invite some of my friends from the college Christian Union to come and experience Pentecostal worship.

But there was just one problem. Although there was usually an interpretation after someone spoke in tongues, there were just one or two occasions when there was not. I was concerned that the friends I invited might get an unfavourable impression and conclude that Pentecostal worship was unscriptural. So I asked a friend, who was a Pentecostal evangelist, what I should do.

That's easy, he said. ***You*** *interpret.*

But I don't have the gift of interpretation, I replied.

Then ask for it, he said.

But how do I know God wants me to have it? I asked.

He then reminded me that we know from Paul's teaching in 1 Corinthians 12-14 that it's God's will for tongues in church to be interpreted, and he suggested that the very fact that I was concerned about it could be an indication that it was a gift God wanted me to have and that I should pray for it[56].

So that's what I did. I began to pray for it, and a few weeks later after someone had spoken in tongues in the Sunday morning meeting and no one else had interpreted it, I spoke out in faith, trusting that the words that had come into my mind were from God. For months I wondered if the gift I had received was genuine, or whether it was 'just me'. Then, one day, at the close of a meeting in which I had interpreted, another Christian came up to me and told me that he had received word for word the interpretation which I had given. I had exercised the gift in faith for months, but finally I had some confirmation that it was real.

About seventeen years later, in November 1977 I was serving as Acting Principal of Mattersey Hall prior to becoming Principal in 1978. One Saturday evening we took a bus-load of about 45 students to Bethshan Tabernacle in Manchester. There were several hundred

---

[56] See 1 Corinthians 14:13.

people in the meeting during which the students sang and testified, and I preached.

As soon as I had finished preaching, a woman near to the back of the meeting began to speak in tongues. As I was still at the microphone, it seemed appropriate for me to interpret so that everyone present would hear and be edified. As usual I spoke out in faith what I felt the Lord had put on my heart. When I had finished, we sang a hymn and the pastor closed the meeting in prayer.

As soon as the meeting was over, one of our students, Guetawende Roamba from Burkina Faso, rushed up to me. He was clearly very excited, and when I asked him what was the matter, he told me that the woman who had spoken in tongues had been speaking his native language. Now in Burkina Faso they speak French, and because I also speak French fairly fluently, I knew that she had not been speaking French. So I wondered what language it might be.

What language? I asked.

Moré, he replied.

Frankly, at that time I had never heard of it – and we found out later that the Irish lady who had spoken in tongues had never heard of it either! But I was excited that I had been present when speaking in tongues had been recognised as a real language. At the same time I was not a little concerned because I was the one who had given the interpretation!

I had been interpreting tongues since I was a student at Oxford in 1960, but it had always been (as it always must be) 'by faith', and yet I still had some intellectual doubts that the gift was genuine. I had simply trusted the promise of Jesus that God gives good gifts to those who ask him (Matthew 7:11). Of course, I had no need to fear, but it's easy to imagine how embarrassed I would have been if I had 'got it wrong' in the presence of one of my Bible College students!

I hardly dared ask the question, but I knew I had to.

And what about the interpretation, Gueta? Was it accurate?

Of course, you know the answer because I wouldn't be telling this story if the interpretation had been wrong! What an amazing thing! The Holy Spirit inspired an Irish woman to speak an African language which she had never heard, or even heard of, and then gave the interpretation to an English man who had never heard of it either! God is faithful. His word is true. And his Spirit is still at work distributing his gifts as he himself determines. The atheists – and for that matter those Christians who say that the gifts are not for today – have no answer to experiences like these.

So it's not surprising that the devil tries to cast doubt on the genuineness of words that we receive from God. He is constantly challenging with words like, *Has God said?* God is more than willing to speak to us, but, if he can, Satan will distract us from listening, or cast doubt on what God has said. But as we step out in faith in what we believe he has said, we will receive confirmation that it is real and learn from experience to recognise that inner voice of God.

CHAPTER SIXTEEN

Other ways God guides us

In PART FOUR we have identified five ways in which God may speak to us directly without involving other people:

- By his audible voice

- By angels

- By dreams and visions

- By supernatural signs

- By promptings, the inner voice of his Spirit

In this chapter we're going to consider other ways in which God may guide us. Throughout this book we've been discussing ways in which God may speak to us. But he sometimes guides us without speaking at all. If we have learned to live by the principles taught in Scripture, we will be guided by them into the right paths. In fact, the more we live by those principles the less we will need the promptings we were talking about in the last chapter.

But, of course, we need both. The principles of Scripture are the general guidelines by which we should live. The promptings of the Spirit are more specific, giving us direction as to what to do in any given situation, but of course they will never conflict with the principles taught in the Bible.

One of the questions that is often asked by young Christians is, *How can I know the will of God?* It's a good question, because as Christians we should certainly want to do his will. In 1 Corinthians 6:19-20 Paul reminds us that we are not our own, we were bought at a price. We belong to God, and we are followers of Jesus who always did God's will[57], even when it meant dying on the cross to save us from our sins

So how can we find the will of God for our lives? Much of the answer to this question is to be found in some of the things we've already said. God's will for our life is that we live in obedience to his word, which is a lamp for our feet and a light on our path (Psalm 119:105). And when we're living in obedience to its teaching, we can expect God to guide us with regard to the specific details. This guidance may come through any of the ways we've already talked about, but the Lord may also be guiding us silently by:

- The trend of circumstances

- Open and closed doors

- The gifts and talents he has given us

- Our total dedication to Jesus

The trend of circumstances
God has a plan for our lives and is constantly working everything out in conformity with the purpose of his will (Ephesians 1:11). He is in complete control of all the circumstances that surround us, even when things appear to be going terribly wrong.

After Stephen was stoned in Acts 7 there was a great persecution of Christians, most of whom fled from Jerusalem and were scattered throughout Judea and Samaria. Some even travelled as far as Antioch

---

[57] Matthew 26:39. Cf. John 4:34, 6:38, Hebrews 10:7

and Cyprus. But as a result there was a revival in Samaria (Acts 8) and a very large church was planted in Antioch (Acts 11:20).

Acts 16:6-10 might well be another example:

> *6 Paul and his companions traveled throughout the region of Phrygia and Galatia, having been kept by the Holy Spirit from preaching the word in the province of Asia.*
>
> *7 When they came to the border of Mysia, they tried to enter Bithynia, but the Spirit of Jesus would not allow them to.*
>
> *8 So they passed by Mysia and went down to Troas.*
>
> *9 During the night Paul had a vision of a man of Macedonia standing and begging him, "Come over to Macedonia and help us."*
>
> *10 After Paul had seen the vision, we got ready at once to leave for Macedonia, concluding that God had called us to preach the gospel to them.*

In obedience to the great commission and God's call upon his life (Acts 9:15, 26:17-18) Paul is on his second missionary journey. So he is already doing the will of God, but he's unsure of where he should go next. Verse 6 tells us that he was *kept by the Holy Spirit from preaching the word in the province of Asia.* We're not told how, but it might well have been through the trend of circumstances.

Next, Paul tries to enter Bithynia, but the Spirit will not allow him to (v7). Then, in the night, he has a vision of a man from Macedonia saying, *Come over to Macedonia and help us* and Paul finally knows what he has to do. It seems that guidance possibly came in three different ways – the trend of circumstances (v6), a word from the Spirit (v7), and a vision in the night (v9).

But although it's not entirely clear how the Holy Spirit told Paul not to go to Bithynia, what's particularly significant in this passage is that Paul gets the guidance he needs while he's already doing what he knows God has called him to do.

This reminds me of Eliezer, Abraham's servant, who in Genesis 24 is sent to look for a wife for Isaac. He makes his way to the town of Nahor and comes to a well just outside the town. He gets his ten camels to kneel down and decides to ask the Lord for a sign. He will ask one of the young women who comes to draw water from the well to give him a drink. But if she's the woman he's looking for, she's to offer to draw water for the camels as well! And, of course, that's what happens!

The story is well-known. But notice what Eliezer says in verse 27. *The Lord has led me on the journey.* Undoubtedly the Lord was leading him throughout his journey, but the specific guidance he needed came well after Eliezer had set out on his journey. In the same way, it's as we get on with the job that God has already given us to do, that we get the guidance we need.

Open and closed doors

Another thing that results from the fact that God is in complete control of circumstances is that he sometimes directs our steps by opening and closing doors. In Revelation 3:7-8 we read:

> *What he opens no-one can shut, and what he shuts no-one can open... See I have placed before you an open door.*

In my final year at Oxford I was praying about what my next step should be. I had been studying for a degree in Philosophy, Politics and

Economics and my plan was now to go to a Bible College to prepare for the ministry God had called me to. So I applied to London Bible College, fully anticipating that they would accept me for their course leading to the London University Bachelor of Divinity Degree.

On the application form, which required me to include a testimony of my Christian experience, I made reference to the baptism in the Holy Spirit. This led to a number of questions at the interview, and it became clear to me that they were suspicious of Pentecostals. So I wasn't entirely surprised when, a few days later, I received a letter saying that they thought I would be happier at a Pentecostal Bible College[58]

Although I felt that their decision was unjust, I reminded myself of the injustice that Joseph had experienced at the hands of his brothers and his recognition later that God had intended it for good (Genesis 37 and 45). God, not the college faculty, had shut the door on LBC. So I considered applying to Kenley, the Assemblies of God Bible College, where Donald Gee, a world-renowned Bible teacher, was then the Principal. So I sent off for the application forms.

However, people were telling me that I didn't need to go to Bible College. I had been preaching since I was fourteen years old, and the Holy Spirit was already using me in teaching and leading others into the experience of the baptism in the Holy Spirit. In those days Assemblies of God did not require any formal training or qualifications for a person to be recognised as a minister. The evidence of one's calling and gifting was fruit from one's ministry. So what should I do?

---

[58]This is well documented in Ian Randall's history of LBC, *Educating Evangelicals.*

I decided that I would go to Kenley unless the Lord opened a door for me to minister in a Pentecostal church. But this seemed highly unlikely because, having grown up in a Baptist church, I was relatively unknown among the Pentecostals and the few churches I had preached in were mostly well provided for with regard to ministry. I told no-one about this decision and yet, a week after making it, I received a letter from the small Assemblies of God Church in Colchester, inviting me to take on the pastorate. And, as if to confirm it, the application form for Kenley that I had asked for never arrived.

Much more recently, my granddaughter Emily asked me to pray for her as she was considering applying to work for Youth for Christ in Birmingham. At the time she was living in London working full time for Alpha and she was uncertain what to do. I assured her that I would pray for her and reminded her of Revelation 3:7-8. I suggested that it might be a good idea to apply for the job and trust the Lord to close or open the door according to his will.

The next day, as Emily was walking in one of the London parks and praying about this, she looked up and saw something she had never seen before – AN OPEN DOOR! It was a piece of modern art, a sculpture of a doorframe with the door within it wide open. The Lord had literally placed before her an open door. Needless to say, she is now working for Youth for Christ in Birmingham.

The gifts and talents God has given us
Another thing that will help us discern the will of God for our lives is having a realistic understanding of the gifts and talents God has given us[59]. In a passage where Paul mentions some of the gifts God has given to his people, he begins by saying:

---

[59] Compare what we said about this in Chapter Six.

For by the grace given me I say to every one of you: do not think of yourself more highly than you ought, but rather think of yourself with sober judgement, in accordance with the faith God has distributed to each of you (Romans 12:3).

Here the emphasis is on not having an exaggerated sense of our own importance, but it's just as important to recognise the gifts and abilities God has given us. Humility does not mean pretending that we're no good at things which in fact we are good at! It means gratefully acknowledging that whatever gifts we do have come from the grace of God.

When Jeremiah protested that he was unsuited for the task God was calling him to, God replied that before Jeremiah was born, he had formed him in his mother's womb (Jeremiah 1:5). Generally speaking, God's will for our lives will be very much in line with the talents he has given us. Those who have heard me sing know very well why I have concluded that it's not God's will for me to be a gospel singer!

Having said that, we know that God can equip a person with supernatural gifts beyond any natural talents they may possess. So, in seeking God's will it's good to ask ourselves what natural talents we have along with any spiritual gifts in which he is using us. But that brings us to by far the most important key to finding the will of God for our lives – our total dedication to Jesus.

Total dedication to Jesus
Still in Romans 12, in the first two verses Paul says:

Therefore, I urge you, brothers, in view of God's mercy, to offer your bodies as living sacrifices, holy and pleasing to God – this is your spiritual act of worship.

193

Do not conform any longer to the pattern of this world, but be transformed by the renewing of your mind. Then you will be able to test and approve what God's will is – his good, pleasing and perfect will.

In these verses Paul shows us how to test what God's perfect will for our lives is. He reminds us of God's love in sending Jesus to die for us and, bearing that in mind, encourages us to live holy, sacrificial lives. We are not to behave as the world behaves or think as the world thinks. We are to be *transformed by the renewing of our minds*. We're to learn to think like God thinks! We're to find out what pleases the Lord (Ephesians 5:10).

If we are seeking to do this, we won't have to worry about finding the will of God. God is perfectly capable of taking care of his own will! The only person or thing that can prevent God's will being done in my life is me! God is all powerful and, by definition, he wants his will to be done.

So as long as I want it to be done, God will make sure that it happens. In short, if we're determined to live all out for Jesus, God will take care of the rest. Sometimes we don't need to know what God's will is, but if we do, he will make it plain. And very often it's as we look *back* over our lives that we see how God has been guiding us all the time, even at times when his voice was silent and it seemed that we were getting no guidance at all. But that may have been simply because we didn't really need it even when we thought we did! But let's finish this chapter with an illustration from the SATNAV system in my car.

Satellite Navigation

These days most cars have some form of satellite navigation system, but, if not, they're readily available as an app on your mobile phone. I've been using them ever since they first became widely available, and my wife, who used to do the navigating when I was driving was immediately thrilled not to have the responsibility. And, to be honest, so was I! But, joking apart, here are some lessons from SATNAV for which the spiritual application should be obvious, although, like most illustrations, the parallel is not always entirely exact.

First, all the SATNAV systems I have had have two things in common. They all have a map you can see and a voice you can hear. For the purpose of these illustrations, let's think of the Bible as the map I can see, and the voice I can hear as the voice of God speaking to me or the guidance of the Holy Spirit.

Bearing that in mind, I have noticed that, whenever I ask for guidance, the map, just like the Bible, is immediately available to me. The voice, on the other hand, is silent until I start my journey. On one system I had, when I was still parked on my drive, the voice would only say, *Guidance will start when you join the highlighted route.*

Another thing I have noticed is that during the journey, although the map is always there for me to look at, the voice is silent until I need to change direction. If I'm travelling on the motorway for two hundred miles, I may not hear the voice for quite a long time!

Finally, I am so glad that if I go off route because I've not been paying attention, both the map and the voice quickly get me back on track. As we've already said, if we really want to go in the right direction, God will make sure that we do.

PART FIVE

HEARING AND RESPONDING

CHAPTER SEVENTEEN

Hearing God's Voice

Throughout this book we've been looking at the many different ways in which God may speak to us. But now it's important that we consider two final things:

- How to **hear** his voice

- How to **respond**.

How to hear God's voice

Although the main purpose of this book has been to answer the question, *How does God **speak** to us today?* an equally important question is, *How can we **hear** his voice?* The answer lies in much of what we have said so far, so my purpose now is to draw together some of those things and add a few further thoughts that I hope will be helpful. We'll begin by outlining some basic facts that we should recognise, using the Bible as our basis.

Recognising the facts

First of all, it's clear from the examples we've looked at in the Bible that **God has a variety of ways of speaking to different people**. Some heard his audible voice, others were visited by angels, while still others had dreams and visions, and so on. God deals with each of us differently.

Why is it, for example, that African Christians are more likely to hear God speak through a dream or vision more easily than British people do? Perhaps it has something to do with our level of expectation. We're all different and I believe that God usually speaks to us in ways that he knows we will recognise as his voice. This may very well mean that he won't speak to you in exactly the same ways that he has spoken to me.

Secondly, the biblical examples we have considered show that the revelations people received were often **totally unexpected** and in some cases were, initially at least, unwanted! Many like Moses and Gideon and Zechariah were just going about their daily business when the Lord appeared to them. God may speak to you when you're least expecting it!

And thirdly, it's clear that most of the cases of God speaking to people in the Bible came at a time when God was calling them to some important task for him, or at **key turning points** in their life or even in history. Obvious examples are:

- Zechariah in Luke 1 before the birth of John the Baptist, the forerunner to the Messiah

- Mary in Luke 2 before the birth of Jesus, the Saviour of the world

- Paul in Acts 9 at his conversion and commissioning for service and in Acts 16 preceding the expansion of the gospel into Europe

- Peter in Acts 10 opening the door of salvation to the Gentiles.

Even for great servants of God like these, such events were not the sort of things that happened every day. So perhaps we should not be too surprised or disappointed if God never speaks to us in such dramatic ways, or if the times he does so are relatively infrequent.

But, of course, there are ways in which we can expect him to speak to us on a regular basis. For example:

- as we read the Bible at home

- through the preaching or prophetic gifts at church

- by the promptings from that voice of the Spirit inside us.

So, recognising these facts, how can we hear God's voice?

Asking, expecting, and listening

Although, as we have seen, God sometimes takes the initiative in speaking to us, there are times when he expects us to begin the conversation with him. James tells us that if we lack wisdom – if we don't know what to do – we should **ask God** and he will gladly give it (James 1:5).

I have already given specific examples from my own experience of how God spoke to me when I asked him to because I urgently needed to know what to do, and I've told you how he wonderfully answered those prayers. On occasions like those, we may well need to make time for God to speak to us, but at others a quick prayer is all that's needed. Although prayer is important, hearing from God does not depend on how much time we spend in prayer. What matters most is how we are developing our relationship with the Lord.

I once heard of a young man whose pastor asked him if he thought God might want him to become a missionary. *Oh no,* he replied, *God hasn't called me.* But then the pastor asked another question:

Are you sure you're within calling distance?

If we've really given our lives wholeheartedly to God, and if we're living in close relationship to him, it will not be difficult for us to hear his voice. We'll always be within earshot. In fact we'll be **expecting** to hear him speak.

Of course, as we've already said, God may very well speak to us when we're least expecting it, as he did very often in the Bible, particularly when he spoke through an angel. But does that mean that we should not expect God to speak to us, but just wait until it happens? Not at all. I believe that every time we read the Bible, or meet together with God's people, we should both ask and expect God to speak to us in one way or another. Sometimes we can miss God's voice because we're not expecting to hear it. And if we're expecting God to speak to us, we'll certainly be **listening**.

Have you ever been in the middle of an important phone call when it's been difficult to hear what the other person is saying because something or someone is distracting you? Maybe you hear a 'ping' alerting you to some notification you've received. Or someone is ringing the doorbell, or someone else has turned on the television. It happens all the time. We're all aware of distractions that prevent us from paying attention to the person who's speaking to us. What do we do in situations like this? Well, if you're like me, you go into another room where it's quiet and free from distractions and where you can listen carefully to what's being said.

I wonder if that's why God so often speaks to us in the night. It's the only time he can get our attention! He wants us to listen, and to do so without distraction. And, if we want him to speak to us, we must make time and find a place when we can pay God the attention he deserves.

Checking we're hearing his voice correctly
Throughout this book we have seen many different ways in which the Lord may speak to us, but whichever way it may be, we need to check that we're really hearing him correctly. This is because we're fallible human beings and, although everything God says is right, it doesn't

necessarily mean that we're hearing it right. Let me remind you of some of the things we've said in earlier chapters.

When we're reading the Bible, which is God's word, we need to make sure that we're understanding it correctly. We need to examine the context to be absolutely sure that the words we are reading directly apply to us. Chapters Three and Four deal with this in some detail. And, when a verse seems to leap out of the page at us, we said in Chapter Six that we should not rely on the words we have read to guide us without seeking confirmation.

In fact, no matter how God speaks to us, we should always look for confirmation that it's really God who is speaking. In 2 Corinthians 11:14 were told that *Satan himself masquerades as an angel of light* and in Galatians 1:8 Paul says:

> But even if we or an angel from heaven should preach a gospel other than the one we preached to you, let him be eternally condemned!

These scriptures remind us that Satan is a deceiver and the only way to avoid being led astray is to test everything against the truth of the gospel as it's revealed in the New Testament. God never contradicts himself, and nothing he says today will contradict what he's already said in his word.

And that's why what we've said already about understanding the Bible correctly is so important. It's not enough to take a single Bible verse as confirmation that it's God who is speaking. We must test it against the whole of Scripture. For example, let's suppose that someone attacks you in the street and as a result you lose the sight of an eye. You're understandably angry about this and a Bible verse comes to mind – *an eye for an eye and a tooth for a tooth*[60]. Does that mean that God is telling you that you should do the same thing to them? Of course not.

There are two good reasons why you should not. First, because even under the law of Moses it is unlikely that these regulations were intended to tell people that they *must* take revenge. It's far more likely that the intention was to teach *proportionate* vengeance. If you've lost an eye, don't take *more than* an eye.

And secondly, and much more importantly, the Lord Jesus said:

> *You have heard that it **was** said, 'Eye for eye, and tooth for tooth.' **But I tell you**, Do not resist an evil person. If someone strikes you on the right cheek, turn to him the other also. And if someone wants to sue you and take your tunic, let him have your cloak as well. If someone forces you to go one mile, go with him two miles. Give to the one who asks you, and do not turn away from the one who wants to borrow from you* (Matthew 5:38-42).

This is a good example of how the whole Bible is to be understood through the lens of the New Testament and in particular in the light of the teaching and character of Jesus. So, if what we're hearing is in keeping with this, then it may well be from the Lord. However, if it's a very specific word of guidance, we need to be sure that it's definitely for us. And, as we saw in earlier chapters, further confirmation can come in various ways, including a strong inner conviction, testing by other Christians, and by time.

---

[60] Exodus 21:24, Leviticus 24:20, Deuteronomy 19:21

Summary

In seeking to hear from God, we need to:

Recognise certain facts

- God may speak to you in a different way than he speaks to me.

- Sometimes God speaks to us when we're least expecting it.

- He will speak most clearly at key turning points in our lives.

- But we can expect him to speak to us on a regular basis as we read the Bible at home, through the preaching or prophetic gifts at church, and by the promptings that come from the voice of the Spirit inside us.

Ask, expect and listen

Sometimes God takes the initiative in speaking to us, but sometimes he expects us to ask him to.

If we're living in right relationship with him, we can expect him to speak to us, especially as we read the Bible etc.

And if we're expecting him to speak, we'll put ourselves in a position to listen.

Check that we're hearing his voice correctly

Satan can masquerade as an angel of light. We need to check that what we're hearing really is the voice of God. We need to make sure that what we're hearing is in line with Scripture and especially with the teaching and character of Jesus.

CHAPTER EIGHTEEN

Responding to God's Voice

So, when we're sure that God has spoken to us, how should we respond? It's a wonderful privilege to know that the Creator of the universe has spoken to you, and our initial response may well be a mixture of surprise, disbelief, awe, excitement, gratitude, and worship. But after this initial reaction, two other things are absolutely vital. We must **believe** what God has said and **do** what he has said.

I mentioned disbelief as part of what might well be our initial reaction, because this was certainly the experience of many of the Bible characters God spoke to – Moses, Gideon, Isaiah, Jeremiah and Ezekiel, for example. So an initial reaction of disbelief, often caused by a very real sense of unworthiness or inadequacy, is quite understandable. But, if we are to do what God says, we must put disbelief behind us and trust that God knows what he's doing! We really have no excuse. Faith comes by hearing the word of God (Romans 10:17) and if God has spoken to us, it's our responsibility to believe it.

But, of course, believing is only the starting point. We must not only believe what God has said to us, we must **do** it. Four times in the Bible we read:

> *Today if you hear his voice, do not harden your hearts*[61]

which in the context relates to disobedience. If God has spoken to us we should not postpone our obedience to his voice. We should believe it and obey it today.

---

[61] Psalm 95:8, Hebrews 3:8, 15; 4:7.

Of course, the specifics of what God says will be different for every reader of this book, but the things that God has said in his word he says to all of us. And one of the great principles I see in Scripture is that **God not only speaks TO us, but he also wants to speak THROUGH us.** In Chapter Ten we showed how God can speak **to** us through spiritual gifts like prophecy, tongues and interpretation[62]. But God can also speak **through** us by these miraculous gifts.

We said earlier that there's a sense in which all God's people are 'prophets'. This doesn't mean that we're all prophets in the Ephesiams 4:11 sense (i.e. like Agabus), or that we all have the spiritual gift of prophecy, but we are all called to speak for God in one way or another.

The Old Testament prophets spoke to God's people, Israel. They also spoke to the heathen nations around them. In a similar way, as God's people today, we Christians are called to speak on behalf of God, not only to our fellow Christians, but also to those around us who do not yet know Jesus. And through the infilling of the Holy Spirit we can receive gifts that will empower us to do that. In fact, without the Holy Spirit's help, we are powerless. And that's why I'm going to conclude by explaining:

- The value of spiritual gifts in encouraging other Christians

- The value of spiritual gifts in evangelism

- How to receive spiritual gifts.

---

[62] And, of course, we could have also mentioned other gifts like words of wisdom and words of knowledge.

The value of spiritual gifts in encouraging other Christians

In 1 Corinthians 12:8-10 Paul lists nine supernatural gifts that are given to Christians as the Holy Spirit determines (v11). In the following verses, using the human body as an illustration of the church and the parts of the body as its members, Paul makes it clear that, though we all have different gifts, we're all needed if the body, the church, is to function properly.

Within the context of the church, the value of these gifts is determined by the extent to which they edify and encourage the members. They are given *for the common good* (1 Corinthians 12:7). And in 1 Corinthians 14:5 Paul says that the person who prophesies is greater than the person who speaks in tongues, unless they interpret, *so that the church may be edified.* Similarly, in Romans 1:11 we read that Paul longed to see the Romans so that he might impart some spiritual gift *to make them strong* (Romans 1:11).

Now in 1 Corinthians 13 Paul makes it clear that, whatever gifts God may give us, they are useless unless our motive is love. He goes on in chapter 14 to emphasise that everything we do as we gather together in church must be for the edification of our fellow Christians (v26). Quite simply, if we really love people, we will want to bless them, and perhaps the best way to do that is to prophesy – to let God speak to them through us. That's why Paul says in 1 Corinthians 14:1:

> *Follow the way of love and eagerly desire the gifts of the Spirit, **especially prophecy**.*

How glad I am for the people who allowed God to speak through them in this way that have proved such a blessing to me over the years. This has usually happened during the course of a service at church, but sometimes it happens privately. In June 2016, totally unexpectedly, Eileen suffered a severe stroke which totally paralysed the right-hand side of her body. Although she made some improvement over the first few months, despite much prayer, six years later she is still unable to walk, and, after the many miracles of healing we have seen, we naturally were asking, *Where is God in all this? Why has she not been healed?*

The answer came through our good friend Barrie Taylor. Barrie and Sandra are the parents of Richard, our daughter Sarah's husband. We only see them about twice a year as they live at quite some distance from us. On one occasion, after a pleasant lunch in a restaurant near our home, Barrie said, *Today I asked the Lord to give me a word for you, and he gave me this:*

> *My Father is at work in your lives and situation, which he is using as a platform to display his sustaining grace.*

It was just what we needed. Despite appearances, God was and is at work in our lives, and although we would love the Lord to heal Eileen – and I still pray that he will – we see regular evidence of his hand at work in ways that would not have been possible if she were fit and well. Each week we have some twenty different carers come into our home and with many of them we have had great opportunities to share the gospel.

But that leads us to the next reason why we should ask the Lord to speak through us prophetically. When we do so, it is not only of great value in encouraging our fellow Christians. It is also a vital component of our telling others about Jesus. And, as we shall see in the next section, the message of the gospel is best proclaimed, not only with **words** given to us by the Spirit, but also by miraculous **deeds** performed by his power.

The value of spiritual gifts in evangelism

Once we have heard and received the good news about Jesus, it's both our privilege and our responsibility to share that good news with others. In John 3:36 Jesus himself gives this warning:

> Whoever believes in the Son has eternal life, but whoever rejects the Son will not see life, for God's wrath remains on him.

It's our privilege to spread the good news that by believing in Jesus we can have eternal life, but it's our serious responsibility to warn people of the dangers of rejecting him. Paul took this responsibility so seriously that he could say in Acts 20:26-27 that he was *innocent of the blood of all men* because he had not hesitated to *proclaim... the whole will of God.*

To use words like these, Paul must have felt his responsibility very strongly. No doubt he had in mind what God had said to Ezekiel when he told him that if he did not warn people of the danger they were in he would hold him accountable for their blood (i.e. their lives)[63]. And it's surely right that we should take our responsibility just as seriously. If someone is lost, don't we need to show them the way? If someone is in danger, don't we need to warn them?

If we genuinely feel that sense of moral responsibility, we will surely want all the help we can get from God to enable us fulfil it. And once we realise that powerful spiritual gifts are available to assist us in this vital task of evangelism, we will surely want to know how to receive them and use them.

---

[63]Ezekiel 3:17-19, cf. 33:2, 6-7

The value of spiritual gifts in evangelism is demonstrated very clearly in the Book of Acts. In Acts 2:41 we're told that about 3000 people became Christians in a single day. This was in response to Peter's preaching, but what had brought such a great crowd under the sound of the gospel was the miraculous gift of tongues (vv4-6).

In Acts 4:4 the number had grown to about 5000, which was the result of the healing of the man who had been lame from birth (Acts 3). In Acts 8:6 we're told that crowds of people in Samaria paid close attention to what Philip said when they saw the miracles he performed, and as a result believed the gospel message and were baptised (v12).

Events like these were a direct fulfilment of Jesus' promise in Mark 16:15-20 where we read:

> He said to them, "Go into all the world and preach the good news to all creation. Whoever believes and is baptized will be saved, but whoever does not believe will be condemned. And **these signs will accompany those who believe: In my name they will drive out demons; they will speak in new tongues; they will pick up snakes with their hands; and when they drink deadly poison, it will not hurt them at all; they will place their hands on sick people, and they will get well.**"

> After the Lord Jesus had spoken to them, he was taken up linto heaven and he sat at the right hand of God. Then the disciples went out and preached everywhere, and **the Lord worked with them and confirmed his word by the signs that accompanied it.**

Here Jesus promises that we can expect spiritual gifts like speaking in tongues, healing, and miracles to accompany the preaching of the gospel. The Christians in the early church recognised this when they prayed in Acts 4:29-31 that God would stretch out his hand to heal and that signs and wonders might be done in the name of Jesus so that God's servants might speak his word with boldness.

And in Romans 15:18-19 Paul could speak of what Christ had accomplished through him in leading the Gentiles to obey God, by what he had said and done

> by the power of signs and miracles through the power of the Spirit,,, So from Jerusalem all the way round to Illyricum I have fully proclaimed the gospel of Christ

which suggests that the gospel is not 'fully proclaimed' unless it is attested by signs from heaven[64].

And although the New Testament largely records miracles that were performed by apostles like Peter and Paul, we should not assume that it's only apostles who can expect to see miracles confirming the word. In the passage we've already quoted, Jesus said,

> These signs will accompany those who **believe** (Mark 16:17).

As believers we are all expected to spread the gospel and we can all expect the Lord to work with us in some way, backing up what we say. As we allow the Lord to speak through us as we tell others about Jesus, we can expect him to work with us confirming the word through whatever spiritual gifts he chooses to give us.

---

[64] For more on this subject, please see, *Just a Taste of Heaven – a biblical and balanced approach to God's healing power,* Chapter 19.

Receiving and using spiritual gifts

1 Corinthians 12:11 tells us that it's the Holy Spirit himself who determines what gifts he should give us. But that does not mean that we cannot put ourselves in a position where we are most likely to receive them. As we draw this book to a conclusion, let me share with you five keys to receiving and using them. They are relevant, not only to spiritual gifts, but also to the whole question of letting God speak to us and through us.

We must desire them eagerly

In 1 Corinthians 14:1 we are told to **eagerly desire** *spiritual gifts*. The Greek verb here is *zeloō*. Paul uses it three times in connection with spiritual gifts. Here, and in 1 Corinthians 12:31 where he encourages the Corinthians to *eagerly desire the greater gifts* by which he probably means those that are of the greatest value in building up the church. See 14:12 where he uses it again.

The verb is a really strong word – the KJV translates it *covet earnestly* – and is the origin of our English word *zeal*. You may remember that one of Jesus' disciples was called Simon the Zealot (Matthew 10:4). The Zealots were a fanatical political group who were determined to overthrow the power of the Romans, no matter the cost. I mention this simply to emphasise the strength of the word that Paul uses to indicate what should be our attitude to spiritual gifts.

So, our starting point, if we want to be used in spiritual gifts, is to ask ourselves how eagerly we desire them – how much we want God to speak to us. Then, the next step will be to stop making excuses.

We must stop making excuses

I'm mentioning this because it's amazing how easy it seems to be to make excuses for not doing the things we know we ought to do. Now I'm not suggesting that every reader will be making all these excuses, and it may be that you're making none of them. But I know from experience that the things I'm going to mention are common causes of Christians not entering into some of the wonderful blessings God has in store for them.

Excuse Number 1   I'm not worthy

The first excuse is quite understandable. In fact, it sounds very spiritual. We know it's wrong to boast, and surely, to say *I'm not worthy* is showing humility? But God doesn't give us these gifts because we deserve them. They come from his **grace**. That's why Paul calls them ***charismata*** (1 Corinthians 12:4) which comes from the word *charis* meaning *grace*.

In fact, everything God gives us comes from his grace. Even the gift of eternal life is a *charisma.* In Romans 6:23 Paul says that *the gift of God is eternal life in Christ Jesus our Lord.* And the word for *gift* here is *charisma.* We don't receive eternal life because we deserve it, but because of God's grace.

And the same is true of spiritual gifts. We receive them despite our unworthiness, or to put it another way, because we have already been made worthy in Christ. The Corinthians are a clear example of this principle. They were not lacking in spiritual gifts (1 Corinthians 1:7), but this was certainly not because they were particularly good

Christians[65]. So we should not hold back from seeking spiritual gifts for ourselves because we are conscious of our own shortcomings.

Excuse Number 2   *I'm not suitable*

This covers a range of excuses – *I'm not talented enough, old enough, clever enough,* and so on. It's here that another word Paul uses can help us. In 1 Corinthians 12:1 he refers to the gifts he's about to talk about as *pneumatika.* The basic meaning of this word is *spiritual,* but in the context it's probably better understood to mean *supernatural.*

As we've said, **all** God's gifts come from his grace, so they're all *charismata.* There are natural gifts and supernatural gifts[66]. Paul refers to the gifts in 1 Corinthians 12:8-10 as *pneumatika* because these particular gifts are supernatural. That means that there's no limit as to the persons God may give them to. They have nothing to do with our natural talents. And they're available to all God's people, irrespective of age, gender, or social status (Acts 2:17ff).

Excuse Number 3   *They're beyond my reach*

Sometimes we're tempted to think that the wonderful gifts we're talking about are somehow beyond our reach. We're conscious of our own humanity and spiritual gifts are manifestations of the supernatural power that comes from God himself. God is in heaven and we are on earth. Surely they're beyond our reach? But no, they are not. **Spiritual gifts do not come from God in outer space!** They come from God who lives **inside you.**

---

[65] See 1 Corinthians 3:3, 5:1-12, 11:21.
[66] Natural gifts include hospitality, marriage, celibacy etc. For a more detailed discussion on this, please see *Body Builders – gifts to make God's people grow,* Appendix.

This is where another word Paul uses to describe these gifts will help us. In 1 Corinthians 12:7 he refers to them as a *manifestation*. The Greek word is *phanerosis* (v7). It comes from a verb meaning *to shine* and has been defined as *a clear display, an outward evidencing of a latent principle*.

To understand this better, please think about a lightbulb. Electricity is the power at work inside it. The light that shines from it is the evidence that the electricity is there. It's a manifestation of the power within. Now think of yourself as the lightbulb, and the Holy Spirit as the power at work inside you, and spiritual gifts as the outward evidence of that power.

It's the Holy Spirit who gives these gifts and he lives inside you. He can manifest through you any gift he chooses. In verse 6 Paul also calls them *energemata,* which literally means *things worked inside*. This means that potentially any of the gifts could be at work in you, because the Giver is already there! But, following our analogy of the lightbulb, it's our responsibility to keep the electricity flowing if the light is to shine. We need to keep filled with the Spirit and the gifts will come.

We must keep filled with the Spirit

In Ephesians 5:18 we're told to be filled with the Spirit. As we saw in Chapter Five, we can best understand what Paul means by this by looking in Acts at the descriptions given there of people being filled with the Spirit. These examples paint a clear picture for us of what Paul means when he tells us to be filled with the Spirit.

We learn from Acts that it's a supernatural experience that is received suddenly rather than gradually and is accompanied by miraculous gifts that greatly empower our witness for Christ. Jesus' first disciples began to exercise the gifts of the Spirit when they were first filled with the Spirit on the day of Pentecost and began to speak in tongues (Acts 2:4)[67]. And if we want to be used in spiritual gifts it's clear that we too need to be filled with the Spirit.

Now the fact that Paul tells us to be filled with the Spirit implies that there is something we can do about it. God's Spirit is always available to us, but it's our responsibility to be filled. In 2 Timothy 1:6-8 Paul says to Timothy:

> For this reason I remind you to **fan into flame** the gift of God, which is in you through the laying on of my hands. For God did not give us a spirit of timidity, but a spirit of power, of love and of self-discipline. So do not be ashamed to testify about our Lord...

There can be no doubt that the 'spirit' referred to in these verses is the Holy Spirit. It's the Holy Spirit who gives us *power* and produces in us fruit like *love* and *self-discipline*. He also enables us to *testify* about the Lord (cf. Acts 1:8). So the *gift of God* that Timothy received through the laying on of Paul's hands was the gift of the Holy Spirit[68].

But what does Paul mean when he tells Timothy to *fan* this gift *into flame*? The Greek word here is *anazopureo*. It literally means *give life again to the fire*. We have the fire of God's Spirit within us, but it's our responsibility to keep it burning. Or, following the analogy we gave earlier, to keep the electricity flowing. And to do that, we need to pray, not only with our mind but also with our spirit, but that's a subject for our next section.

---

[67] For more on what it means to be filled with the Spirit, please see *A New Dimension – How to be filled with the Holy Spirit*
[68] Compare Acts 8:17, 19:6

We must pray

Talking about spiritual gifts in 1 Corinthians 14:12-15, Paul says this:

> ¹² *So it is with you. Since you are eager to have spiritual gifts, try to excel in gifts that build up the church.*

> ¹³ *For this reason anyone who speaks in a tongue should pray that he may interpret what he says.*

> ¹⁴ *For if I pray in a tongue, my spirit prays, but my mind is unfruitful.*

> ¹⁵ *So what shall I do? I will pray with my spirit, but I will also pray with my mind; I will sing with my spirit, but I will also sing with my mind.*

In verse 12 Paul acknowledges that the Corinthians are eager to have spiritual gifts, but he wants them to concentrate on gifts that build up the church. He is emphasising something he's already said in verses 1-5 where he makes it clear that prophecy is more valuable for the church than speaking in tongues. Tongues are useful for personal edification (v4), but prophecy will edify the church. However, tongues can be a means of edifying the church, but only if it's accompanied by the gift of interpretation (v5).

So, in verse 13 he says that anyone who speaks in a tongue should pray that they may interpret what they are saying. That way the church will be edified as well as the person speaking in tongues. And, apart from anything else, this verse shows us that, if we're eagerly desiring a spiritual gift (v12), we should **pray** for it.

Paul then goes on in verses 14-15 to tell us something very important about speaking in tongues. Although, as we've seen, it's of no value to the church unless it's interpreted, it's of great value to the individual Christian. He says that when we pray in tongues we are praying *with the spirit*. This is different from praying *with the mind* which is what we do when we pray in English (or any other language we have learned).

So if we pray in tongues we are praying with our spirit. This is not a reference to the Holy Spirit, although of course it's the Holy Spirit who enables us to speak in tongues. When I pray in English, I understand what I'm saying, but when I pray I tongues I do not. But, even so, Paul says it edifies me (v4).

So, Paul says in verse 15:

> *What shall I do? I will pray with my spirit, I will also pray with my mind.*

This clearly shows his determination to do both. And if we are to *fan into flame* the gift of the Spirit, we need to too. Like Jackie Pullinger, who testifies that speaking in tongues for fifteen minutes a day has resulted in her seeing amazing miracles among drug addicts in Hong Kong, spiritual gifts will happen in our lives as we fan into flame the gift of the Spirit within us. We need to keep filled with the Spirit by praying with our spirit (in tongues) and praying with our understanding (in English) specifically asking for spiritual gifts, as Paul encourages the Corinthians in verse 13, for example.

But how do I know what to pray for? Aren't the gifts distributed as the Holy Spirit determines? And what if I start asking for a gift that it's not his will for me to have? These are the kind of questions my students often asked me, and I quite understand why. But the problem is, if we don't know what to pray for, we probably won't pray for any of them.

As I was thinking and praying about the best way to answer these questions, I felt the Lord say to me,

> Tell them to pray for whatever gift they like. I'm delighted they're praying for any of the gifts. I will direct them as they continue to pray.

I quickly saw the Lord's wisdom in giving that advice. All God's gifts are good, and it's good to pray for any of them. But if the gift we're asking for is not for us, the Lord will soon move us towards the ones that are. As we said in Chapter Sixteen, God usually guides us when we're on the move. Remember the illustration of the SATNAV?

It's also helpful to remember that, when we don't know what to pray for as we pray with our mind (in English), if we pray with our spirit (in tongues), not understanding what we are saying, the words we speak in tongues may well be voicing a request for the very gifts God is planning to give us.

We must act in faith

So, if we're *eagerly desiring* for God not only to speak **to** us, but also to speak **through** us, if we've *stopped making excuses*, if we're keeping *filled with the Spirit*, and if we're *praying* that God will give us these wonderful gifts, all we need to do now is *act in faith*.

Jesus himself said that gifts like tongues, healings and miracles would accompany those who *believe* (Mark 16:17-18), and the apostle Paul tells us that those who prophesy should do so in accordance with their *faith* (Romans 12:6). And James tells us that *faith without works is dead* (James 2:17). We have to **do** something. If we want God to speak through us, **we** have to **speak**.

221

An example of this is how I began to exercise the gift of interpreting tongues, which I've already told you about in Chapter Fifteen. I acted in faith, despite my doubts. Now I know that may sound like a contradiction. Can faith and doubt really coexist? Yes, because where there is no room for doubt there is no need for faith. I don't need faith to believe that 2+2=4 because there's no room for doubt about it.

It's rather like courage and fear. Courage is only needed when there is something to fear, and as Nelson Mandela once said:

> *I learned that courage was not the absence of fear, but the triumph over it. The brave man is not the one who does not feel afraid, but he who conquers that fear.*

Similarly, faith is not the absence of doubt. It's acting despite any doubts you may have, because you know you can trust the Lord. He doesn't give stones or scorpions or snakes when we ask for the Holy Spirit (Luke 11:11-13) or when we ask for his gifts (Matthew 7:9-11). Trusting in these promises, we can act in faith, knowing that God will not let us down.

But finally, one more very important thing needs to be said. Throughout this book we have been talking about how God speaks to us, and in this final chapter we've been considering how he wants speak through us, how we can speak for him. And we've used spiritual gifts as an example of how we can do this. But as we said in Chapter One when we were considering the example of the Lord Jesus, God speaks to us through him, not only by the things he said, but by the kind of person he was. He speaks through his life. And the same is true for us. Perhaps the most powerful way that God can speak through any of us is through our lives. That's why, greater than any spiritual gift is the fruit of love.

Conclusion

My purpose in this book has been to show how God speaks to us today and how we can recognise his voice. The Bible, God's written word, has been the basis for all we have said, but wherever possible I have sought to illustrate its truth by examples from my own life and experience. Now, in the conclusion, it seems appropriate to summarise what we have discovered.

In the INTRODUCTION we saw that God speaks to all humankind by his **creation**. We said that the world we live in, and the heavens above, are clear evidence that a wonderful designer has been at work. We referred to passages like Psalm 19:1-4 and Romans 1:20 to show that, as far as the Bible is concerned, we have no excuse for not believing in God. And the creation speaks eloquently, not only of God's existence, but of his great and glorious power, his wisdom, his faithfulness, his beauty and his love[69].

But these divine qualities are seen much more clearly in **the Lord Jesus Christ,** through whom God has finally spoken to us in the person of his Son (Hebrews 1:1-2). In PART ONE we saw that God speaks to us through the *person* of Jesus revealing what God is like, in the *words* of Jesus teaching us what to believe, and in the actions of Jesus showing us how to behave.

In PART TWO we examined how God speaks to us through the **Bible.** We began by giving reasons why we should believe that God speaks in this way[70]. We then gave important guidelines on how to understand the Bible correctly[71] and in Chapter Four we talked about how to identify, understand, and receive God's promises.

---

[69] See Introduction
[70] Chapter 2
[71] Chapter 3

But there's more to the Bible than promises. God gives us instructions, showing us what to believe and how to behave. He does this through the person, the words and the actions of Jesus, the direct teaching found in the New Testament, and by examples from the lives of God's people[72]. Finally, in Chapter Six we saw how God sometimes directs us by bringing key verses to our attention.

In PART THREE we considered how God often uses **other people** to speak to us, including parents, other Christians, preachers and pastors, prophets and prophecy.

And in PART FOUR we looked at ways in which God speaks to us directly without using other people. We gave examples from the Bible and, where possible, from personal experience, of God speaking with an **audible voice, through angels, by dreams and visions, supernatural signs, and by promptings, the voice of his Spirit within us.**

Then we thought about some of the **ways God guides us silently.** We saw that he may do so through the trend of circumstances, by opening and closing doors, and through the gifts and talents God has given us. But ultimately, if we really want to discover God's perfect will for our lives, we must make sure that our minds are constantly being renewed so that we think like God thinks and are willing to present our bodies as a living sacrifice to him (Romans 12:1-2),

Finally, in PART FIVE, we saw that God wants to speak **through** us as well as **to** us. One way that he does this is through spiritual gifts, and we examined what the Bible teaches about their importance in building up God's people and in evangelism. We then considered how we can best put ourselves in a position to receive these gifts by eagerly desiring them, realising that our receiving them is not

---

[72] Chapter 5

dependent on our own goodness, talents or abilities. We stressed our responsibility to keep filled with the Spirit, to pray, and to act in faith. As we do these things we will surely come to know the joy of recognising God's voice when he is speaking to us, and of allowing him to speak through us to others.

One final word. It's important to realise that it's highly unlikely that God is going to speak to any of us in **all** the ways mentioned in this book. Some of the things we've talked about are quite unusual – the appearance of angels or hearing the audible voice of God, for example. And we mustn't assume that these forms of communication are in some way superior to the other ways God speaks to us.

So don't be disappointed if you never see an angel or hear God's audible voice. Rather, let him speak to you regularly as you read the Bible every day, as you pay attention to the preaching of his word and to the exercising of spiritual gifts in church, and as you listen to those promptings that come from God's Spirit within you.

To listen to the teaching found in this book, please visit:
www.davidpetts.org
which gives details of a series of
22 PODCASTS
titled
HOW GOD SPEAKS TO US TODAY

Other helpful books by David Petts

If you'd like to explore this subject more, the following books are available from my website where a more detailed description of each book may be found.

The Holy Spirit – an Introduction

For a more detailed look at the person and work of the Holy Spirit this book is a must. It deals with the Spirit in the Old and New Testaments, the Spirit in the teaching of Jesus, the Spirit in the believer, the fruit and gifts of the Spirit, the Spirit in the church, and the Holy Spirit in the future.

Body Builders – gifts to make God's people grow

A detailed look at spiritual gifts in the New Testament, examining particularly the gifts listed in Ephesians 4:11 and those in 1 Corinthians 12:8-10. This book will help you understand what these gifts are and how to receive them.

Signs from Heaven – why I believe

A short book intended as an evangelistic tool containing testimonies of miracles from my own experience.

Just a Taste of Heaven – a biblical and balanced approach to God's healing power

As the title suggests, this book is about healing. Part One deals with biblical passages on healing. Part Two presents a positive but balanced theology of healing and Part Three offers practical guidelines for ministering to sick people with examples of miracles of healing from my own experience. If you want to be used in healing, I encourage you to read this book.

You'd Better Believe It!

20 chapters on basic Christian doctrine with study questions at the end of each chapter. Suitable for personal study or for use in home-groups.

How to Live for Jesus

Intended for new Christians, this book contains 10 short chapters on living the Christian life.

For more details on any of these books, visit:

www.davidpetts.org

L - #0446 - 281122 - C0 - 210/148/13 - PB - DID3432246